CN01270767

TO

ON

TOUR

VIVA ESPAÑA

Written by

The Brontë Mumma

Grosvenor House
Publishing Limited

All rights reserved
Copyright © Francesca L McLinden, 2025

The right of The Brontë Mumma to be identified as the author of
this work has been asserted in accordance with Section 78
of the Copyright, Designs and Patents Act 1988

The book cover is copyright to The Brontë Mumma
All interior artwork and cover design by The Brontë Mumma,
in collaboration with The Daisy Design Studio
With the exception of three images, copyright to: Kristofer Keane,
BearFotos and Jose Carrasco, courtesy of Shutterstock

This book is published by
Grosvenor House Publishing Ltd
Link House
140 The Broadway, Tolworth, Surrey, KT6 7HT.
www.grosvenorhousepublishing.co.uk

This book is sold subject to the conditions that it shall not, by way of
trade or otherwise, be lent, resold, hired out or otherwise circulated
without the author's or publisher's prior consent in any form of
binding or cover other than that in which it is published and
without a similar condition including this condition being
imposed on the subsequent purchaser.

A CIP record for this book
is available from the British Library

ISBN 978-1-80381-932-7
eBook ISBN 978-1-80381-933-4

To my musketeers- d'Adtagnan and Bronthos.
With much love and thanks,
Maramis

With all good wishes,
Francesca Mclinda
The Brontë Mumma

THE MAP

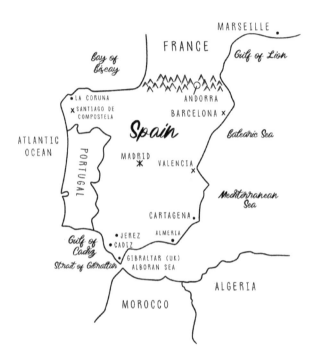

Here is a helpful map of Spain. It features the places that we visited and a few others that we didn't. It's not to scale, so those in the geographical know, please forgive a little bit of cartographical artistic licence.

HELLO

This is a travelogue. But don't worry, it's not a boring one. I've intentionally chosen to leave the duller parts out and instead, bequeath you with little nuggets of greatness. Along the way, you'll find a few fascinating facts thrown in for good measure, as well as an honest account of what it's like to travel as a one year old with parents. This is where my travelogue is unique. It is told through eyes that are a lot lower down than those of the adult of the species. Everything is new to me- even ancient monuments, which is very useful when you are a travel novice, because every little thing is simply amazing.

I'll be honest with you. I'm still finding my feet as a junior member of the human race and learning as I go. It's not easy, navigating life when there's no manual and you've got parents to supervise. However, each day is a fascinating insight into the world and its people. Add an adventure into the mix and the fascination steps up a notch. Pull on your specs, switch to channel Brontë and join me and the folks as I take you on a thrilling expedition in *Toddler on Tour: Viva España*.

HOLIDAY PALM

THE ITINERARY

03 September - Goodbye England - depart Southampton

04 September - Sailing the seven seas

05 September - Hello land- La Coruna

06 September - Bobbing along the ocean

07 September - More ocean bobbing

08 September - Land ahoy- Valencia

09 September - More land- Cartagena

10 September - At sea

11 September - In port- Hōla Barcelona

12 September - Take two- Barcelona beckons

13 September - Sea legs

14 September - Final Spanish stop - Cadiz

15 September - Ocean bound

16 September - Sailing North

17 September - Hello England - Southampton awaits

INTERRUPTED GENIUS
AT WORK

A SORT-OF DISCLAIMER

What you are about to read is the truth, the whole truth, and nothing but the truth. Kind of. You see, I'm a one year old and do not yet possess the ability to articulate everything that happens, neither do I have the means of communicating all such happenings. As you may well imagine, I am not yet operational in the art of the pen. For the record though, I can create some excellent scribbles that often continue off of the paper and onto the canvas all around me. Said canvas is generally what the parents refer to as 'the floor'. At that point, my tools are swiftly confiscated.

Linguistically speaking, I'm limited to a small and exclusive collection of words that I'm able to verbalise. But in my mind, wow. There is a whole encyclopaedia of knowledge up there. Fortunately for me, ever since I was born into the world, Mummy and I have shared a very strong meeting of minds. We're pretty much telepathic, which made documenting this voyage a lot easier. We're on the same wavelength, which is actually a real thing. Neuroscience boffins have researched it extensively and proved it. But to try to make it sound more fancy and scientific, they call this bond 'brain coupling'. So, through the coupling of our brains, I have been able to pour my thoughts along the Brontë-Mumma Invisibond, all the way into Mummy's fingertips and the book that you are now holding.

I have titled this book *Viva España*, because it is the thrilling tale of my odyssey to Spain and my first time abroad. My second choice of title was *The Almost Circumnavigation of Spain*, because we almost circumnavigated the perimeter of Spain. We basically did a giant horseshoe around the country, starting in the northwest and then skirting the shores of Portugal, continuing all the way up to the quirky Catalan capital city of Barcelona on the northeastern side of the country. Obviously, we didn't manage to circle the entirety of Spain as this would have meant a significant detour onto land and an expedition through the Pyrenees, skirting the edge of France. Apparently, this would not have been toddler compatible. So, we remained on our ocean-going vessel and went around the outside sea borders. Maybe when I'm a bit older we'll trek across the Pyrenees. When we left England, I was only able to manage about three or four tottery steps before falling over. Of course, I had my other means of transportation: the crawl and the bottom shuffle, but to put those into operation on a jaunt through the Pyrenees would have taken forever and a day.

LET'S P&O CRUISE AS WE'RE READY TO SCHMOOZE

In the spirit of sharing, here's some more helpful information. It might be worth knowing this before you board the book and embark on our adventure.

Cruise liner - *P&O Cruises*

Ship - Arvia

Holiday number - K318

Holiday duration - 14 nights

Embarkation - Southampton

Disembarkation - Southampton

Destinations - La Coruna, Valencia, Cartagena, Barcelona for two days, Cadiz

P&O Cruises is a behemoth of the cruising world. It started operating in 1837, so I would have been aged minus 185. I was so far into the future that I wasn't even a blip, let alone a thought that had crossed anyone's mind. 1837 was a year of great change as it marked the start of Queen Victoria's reign, when she took over the mantle of monarch at the tender age of eighteen. At the same time, the beginning of *P&O Cruises'* commercial enterprise began with a steamship carrying mail to the Iberian Peninsula when the company was known as the *Peninsular Steam Navigation Company*. The Iberian Peninsula is made up of several countries: Spain, Portugal, Gibraltar, Andorra and a smidge of France. That said, it's mainly associated with Spain and Portugal. So it feels like our holiday is a retracing of a historic journey that mirrored the start of *P&O Cruises'* early routes. Although, I'm sure that our accommodation was probably a lot more comfortable and luxurious than that of a steamship designed to carry letters and parcels.

Over the following years, *P&O Cruises* grew and expanded. It branched out from mail and had forays into cargo and cruising, as well as stints of national service during wartime. Now, in the present day, *P&O Cruises* has been merged with the *Carnival Corporation* in 2003.

The current *P&O Cruises* fleet is made up of seven iconic ships painted white with the striking red, white and blue, of the union jack incorporated into each vessel. The ships in the fleet are Arvia, Azura, Britannia, Iona and Ventura, as well as Arcadia and Aurora. The first five are family friendly and the last two are exclusively for adults. We sailed on the newest ship, Arvia, who had her maiden voyage on

23 December 2022 after being constructed in a shipyard in Germany that began trading in 1795. Unlike Arvia, I was not built in the *Meyer Werft* shipyard in Papenburg. No, I was made in Mummy's tummy some 535 miles (862 km) to the south west of Papenburg on the Isle of Wight, off the south coast of England.

WHO'S WHO IN THE TRAVEL PARTY?

We are a happy trio made up of me, Mummy and Daddy. I like to think of us as three magnificent musketeers. We have followed in the footsteps of Athos, Aramis and d'Artagnan. Through no fault of his own, Porthos did not make the cut. Inspired by Dumas and his literary heroes, I have bestowed the new musket-less musketeers for the modern family with fitting name tributes. I, Brontë, am of course Bronthos. Thank you Athos. Mummy is Maramis. And for obvious reasons, Daddy is d'Adtagnan.

So you know a little more about me and my travel companions, I have listed some essential information. This includes a list of alternative names that may feature in the travelogue, our ages, distinguishing features, hobbies, and anything else that might be useful to know.

Brontë

Other names - Mrs Bongles/ Bronthos/ The Boss (only joking. I wish)

Age - 15 months when we left Southampton and 16 months when we returned

Distinguishing features - Curly hair, free of clips and accessories because they get in the way and stuck on things/ likes to smile lots/ blue eyes

Hobbies - Hiding things that Mummy and Daddy need/ playing with anything that isn't actually mine/ walking/ getting up to mischief/ splashing in the bath/ waving/ making music/ keeping Mummy and Daddy on their toes (known as bongling, after my nickname of Mrs Bongles)

Anything else - My Mummy and Daddy are my favourite people in the world. My favourite food is jelly and I love to start and end the day with a dash of milk

Mumma

Other names - Mummy/ Maramis/ The Captain (only joking. Mummy wishes)/ The Parents (one half of)

Age - Older than me

Distinguishing features - Straight hair/ taller than me/ likes smiling (especially at me)

Hobbies - Washing and ironing/ playing the piano/ writing and pretending to be a world famous author

Anything else - Likes exploring and discovering new things. That's lucky, because I do too and because I'm still quite new to the world, I discover new things all the time. I'm a proper explorer

Dadnad

Other names - Daddy/ Naddad/ d'Adtagnan/ The Lieutenant (only joking. Daddy wishes)/ The Parents (the other half of)

Age - Older than Mummy

Distinguishing features - Wavy hair/ taller than Mummy/ kind eyes that can magically have x-ray vision and sense when I am about to embark on a mischief streak

Hobbies - Talking to me and Mummy/ walking/ playing games with me/ reading

Anything else - Daddy is my official nap buddy

SUPERNANA'S CAPE

02 September

EMPTY SUITCASES

I go on holiday tomorrow. I'm told that's quite exciting. Although, I don't actually know what a holiday is. That said, I have so far deduced that it involves Mummy rushing around the house, moving random items from one place to another. It also involves empty suitcases being retrieved from the loft and taunting me with their open invitation to use them as a climbing frame. I am perplexed by something though. Why are we bringing cases for suits, when none of us wear suits? It gets even more peculiar when you think that suitcases were preceded by trunks. And no, they were not attached to an elephant. Let me rephrase things. I'm not going to call our clothes-carrying bags suitcases or trunks, because both options feel a bit like false advertising. I will go with the more accurate descriptor of luggage, because Daddy is going to have to lug it along.

Nana came round to see me and Mummy while Daddy was finishing his work. She asked Mummy if we were all packed and ready to go, to which Mummy replied that she was 'packed in her mind'. In other words, the answer was no. At this point, I then shuffled across to Nana and turned to face Mummy as I didn't want to bask in Nana's gaze of incredulous bemusement that was casting a hazy glow over Mummy. Being on the Nana side gave me a bit more kudos and made me less complicit in the empty clothes vessel situation, even though their lack of contents was partly my fault. I am- after all, what I affectionately like to term; a glorious distraction. Why do sensible grown-up things when your time could be better spent in play? Or going to the library, for a walk in the park, or swimming? Usually, Nana would agree with me completely, but today was no ordinary day because we were off on an expedition in less than 24 hours with nothing but the clothes that we were wearing, a months' supply of nappies (just in case. In case of what, I never had clarified), some sunglasses, my pushchair, and an abundance of dried snacks.

Nana put her cape on and Supernana arrived to take control of the situation. We reconvened to my bedroom and all of a sudden, the wardrobe doors were thrown wide open and the contents of my drawers were sent flying through the air before landing neatly in my bag. Whilst Mummy and Supernana were having a serious discussion about how much swimwear I would need, I saw a window of opportunity and firmly grasped it with both hands. My half-full luggage was unattended, so I started helping and removing everything that I felt was surplus to requirements. Mummy and Supernana quickly reached a conclusion about my swimming garb and turned their attentions back to me. As it turns out, they didn't want my assistance, so I was then banished to my cot and sentenced to watch proceedings from a metre further away. Not long later, my holdall graduated from luggage and emerged as my baggage, as luggage becomes baggage once it's filled with one's worldly wares.

During a well-earned tea and milk break, we spotted a boat on the sea that wasn't a). a French car ferry, b). a fishing boat, c). a cruise liner, d). a sailing vessel, or e). another French car ferry. No, as part of its summer circuit around the coastline of the Isle of Wight, the *Waverley* paddle steamed into view, immediately transporting us back to the days of yesteryear. With her two distinctive funnels and side paddles creating a frothy white wake around it, the *Waverley* invited us to say 'hello nostalgia'. Quickly Nana went to grab her phone to take a few pictures, but by the time she'd retrieved it from the depths of her cavernous handbag, the steamer was not much more than a boat backside. Considering that the *Waverley* was brought into commission in 1946 and is the worlds last seagoing paddle steamer, she can certainly move at a rate of knots. As she disappeared around Woody Bay, we finished our beverages and then Nana and I set to important matters involving playing whilst Mummy got to the business of packing stuff for her and Daddy. And then, just like that, we were holiday ready.

The iconic Waverley paddle steamer at sea
(sadly, we are not in this picture).

03 September

SLEEP IS
FOR LOSERS

SUNRISE 06:22
SUNSET 20:43

As I write this, it is close to midnight and we are in the open waters of the English Channel, heading towards the Atlantic Ocean. I know that we're no longer off the shores of England as Mummy and Daddy's mobile phones have tuned into a different maritime network that costs about five thousand Earth pounds a minute to use. Swiftly, the telephones were switched off and relegated to the safe. With full steam ahead, Captain Camby sailed us out of the 46,602 square miles (75,000 km^2) of water that makes up the English Channel and into the mouth of the Atlantic with its 41,105,000 square miles (106.5 million km^2) and forty-three species of shark. Huddled in our cabin, we felt very small and the boat very big. But when I think that the Atlantic covers 17% of the Earth's surface, I realised that we weren't just small, we were atom sized in relation to the seas we were about to venture into.

In the big scheme of things, we didn't travel that far to get to Southampton. I almost feel slightly embarrassed to write that it's been a long day and that I'm rather tired, especially when I've heard hardy, weary people saying that they spent eight or eleven hours respectively, on a coach to get here. It took us a couple of hours to make the 27 mile journey (43 km). The roads weren't overly busy, but given that our journey involved a catamaran trip, there was lots of loading and unloading of me and the baggage from car to boat to taxi to giant ship.

From the Isle of Wight we crossed the 20 mile long (32 km) stretch of water that makes up The Solent and then took a taxi to the *Ocean Cruise Terminal* in Southampton. I was excited to learn that, sailing into Southampton in 1840 was the first *P&O Cruises* passenger ship. Yet, Southampton has been a port since the Roman era and today welcomes over 2 million people annually. That's roughly 1.999 million more people than I know.

I woke up feeling bright and refreshed at 7 am and ready to face the trials and tribulations of the day ahead, which is just as well because bed did not beckon me until gone 10:30 pm. That, ladies and gents, is very late for me these days. When I was new to the world and had youth on my side, I could easily party on through until 4 am. But now, as a senior baby, I do need my beauty sleep. If I don't get it, I'm in danger of becoming a grumple. That said, in my defence, I didn't actually intend to stay up so late, and neither did the parents. Quite frankly, I don't know how I managed to keep my eyes open for so long as my one solitary nap today was no more than a generous half an hour whilst in the car and in transit to the ferry. I ask you, can you call a nap 'a nap', if it is less than ninety minutes? I would say not.

Through no fault of the parents (or my own), I was denied quality rest time. Yet somehow, we discovered I had energy reserves that appeared as the day progressed. I don't know where I stored said energy reserves, but they kept me going until long after dark. In the end, when I'd reluctantly succumbed to the allure of sleep, Mummy retired to the bathroom whilst Daddy had a night time stroll and I contemplated some of life's great mysteries like, is it normal to be longer than your bed? And why is it easier for me to walk on a ship at sea than it is on land? I know, they're deep. Like seven leagues of the sea, type deep.

Grandpa very kindly picked us up at home and drove us to the passenger boat in Cowes (no, not named after the bovine animals, but quite possibly some old sandbanks). We crossed The Solent using the *Red Jet*, which is the passenger ferry arm of *Red Funnel*. In 1820, the first steamer service was established between Cowes and Southampton. Fast-forward a few years and we get to 1861- the year that Prince Albert died. He spent a fair amount of time on the Isle of

Wight with Queen Victoria and their children at Osborne House. In the same year, the *Southampton Isle of Wight and South of England Royal Mail Steam Packet Company Limited* launched. At some point in time, somebody had the good sense to rechristen the company as *Red Funnel*, after the red funnels of their ships.

After Grandpa had dropped us off at the boat, we zipped across The Solent where I was liberally plied with savoury biscuit snacks and melty buttons. I knew it was a bribe to buy my silence, but damn, Mummy's good. She knows I just can't resist a dried baked good. Well played mother, well played.

On the Mainland (also known as England), I had my first taxi experience. I sat on Mummy's lap and talked gibberish with Dad. It wasn't a long trip. To be precise, it was £7-80 worth of long. Really, it only needed to be £5-20, but the taxi driver decided to wait at a zebra crossing with about thirty senior citizens and their luggage. That meter kept on rolling as the wheels on their suitcases slowly cranked into second gear. But once we'd vacated the taxi, we deposited the bags, checked in, and then boarded the gigantic Arvia.

In Latin, Arvia actually means 'from the seashore', which is rather fitting for an ocean liner, but if you're not in the know with Latin, it may as well mean 'huge, gargantuan vessel', because Arvia is colossus and holds over 5,000 guests, including me, Mummy and Daddy. Interestingly, the captain of this rather substantial ship- Mr Robert Camby, is the same chap that captained Azura, the boat that Mummy and Daddy boarded for their honeymoon back in 2016. It's a small world.

From up on deck 16, we ventured to the starboard side of the ship and surveyed the port and surrounding area. Out of the blue, we watched as the *Waverley* steamed into view with her backward leaning funnels across the waters that were as calm and gentle as a millpond. You wait for years to see a paddle-steamer and then you see the same iconic ship- twice, in a 24 hour window.

Nostalgia collided with modern luxury in a funny old turn of events. At our disposal, we had the opulence of a £700 million ship beneath our feet and all around us. Yet the thing that caught our attention was the little slice of history with its tiny ant-sized passengers enthusiastically waving up at us on this shiny new boat. As we watched the *Waverley* disappear into the distance, time seemed to slow as the low cloud with the setting sun erased the giant cranes and port machinery from our vision and brought our focus squarely onto this floating wonder that was gifted to the *Waverley Preservation Society, Ltd,* for the princely sum of £1-00 in 1974. I don't know much about money, but I do know that that is one heck of a bargain.

Once aboard Arvia, we had a bite to eat in the self service restaurant and then went to find our room-sorry, cabin. There's a lot of wow's coming your way.

Wow! We must be important as we're at the very front of the ship. Daddy's planning on being a backseat driver. I'll keep him company.

Wow! This ~~room~~ cabin is compact. I've got shoeboxes bigger than this place.

Wow! The walls and ceilings are magnetic. Who knew? I thought that was just a wild rumour.

Wow! There's no bed for me. Where do I sleep? Hmm. This crucial piece of furniture is noticeably absent. Perhaps I'll be upgraded to the Mummy and Daddy bed? Nope. No such luck.

Wow! They've brought me a bed. I don't want to seem ungrateful, but it's the worlds smallest travel cot and I appear to be longer than it. Luckily, I like to sleep like a concertinaed frog, compact and parcelled up into myself. That said, I do like a good stretch and roll. I may have to abandon the downward dog in favour of the folded mouse.

Our cabin was bijou. It had a bed fit for a queen. Or at least I'm assuming that's what queen size means? You know what else this suggests? My Mummy must be a queen. So that makes me a princess. What a result. I've gone from a regular citizen to royalty since entering this cabin. Wowie indeed.

In addition to the bed, there was built-in wardrobes, a sofa that could be a bed, a very useful mini-fridge, a desk area with chair, and a wall-mounted television. The big glass door led to our steel fronted balcony in the forward of the ship. (Look at me, all up to speed with the lingo. Forward means the front). We had an ensuite shower room with my baby bath stashed inside the shower cubicle. Over the next couple of weeks, Mummy would become very accustomed to the floor of the bathroom when she was trying to get her daily writing fix squeezed in, without disturbing me with the scratch of the pen gliding over the page.

Once the pushchair was parked in the hallway of our cabin, there wasn't that much space. And when my bed arrived, the doorway to the balcony was decommissioned and relegated to 'out of action' when I was in the baby bed.

I should probably add that if it was just d'Adtagnan and Maramis on holiday, the cabin would have been plenty big enough for them. Considering I'm such a little person, I come with a lot of equipment, and that equipment's got to find a home. Luckily, there was swathes of empty space under the bed, begging to be filled.

Apparently, once a year, the ship has a muster station gathering. I don't know if it was good luck or unfortunate timing, but our trip coincided with the annual muster announcement. We had to sit in the theatre and be shown how to put a life jacket on, as demonstrated by the cap and yellow life-jacket wearing crew. We also had to listen to seven alarm bells, followed by one long one. This is sounded in the event of danger. But if you are in danger, having to count the seven short blasts and wait for the loud, long dong confirming that you are *definitely* in mortal peril, would be quite stressful. And what happens if you lost count?

I kept those thoughts to myself as the presentation was so boring I was unable to resist the urge to rest my eyes. (The resting of ones eyes does not equate to napping. Mummy has confirmed this ruling for me). Sadly, I am unable to tell you if we were in any real danger as I lost count of how many alarms sounded.

After dinner, we ambled on back to our ~~room~~ cabin and *hallelujah!*, our bags had finally arrived. It was gone 8 pm by this time, which was quite late for a suitcase reunion. It was a big relief to have our things as my milk and pyjamas were stashed in there. Hastily, the parents fished out my milk and I had not one, but two bottles of the good stuff. It's thirsty work being a bongle and having to be adored by so many strangers who all seemed compelled to try to touch my hair.

Following my double shot of milk, I folded myself like a piece of origami into my cot and went straight to meet with the supervisor of Brontë Dreamland Productions.

COUSIN JUAN OF THE SPANISH FARM

04 September

SOMEWHERE NEAR BISCAY AND ITS BAY

SUNRISE 07:40
SUNSET 20:59

Either we musketeers were super sleepy yesterday, or the blackout curtains are so effective as to render the sunrise obsolete, that without an alarm we could have slept on through to midday. They say that if you snooze, you lose. And lose we did as our plans for the morning were swiftly gobbled up by Xixili, the mythical nymph with a pair of duck feet on her tail, who emerged in the blink of an eye on the crest of a crashing wave from within the murky depths of Biscay. I know, it's a pretty dramatic way to say that we overslept. By accident. Our intentions were good, but those blackout curtains led us off the strait and narrow path of good intentions.

What happened is really quite simple. Mummy and Daddy should have known better, but they've been out of the travel fold on account of the pandemic pausing life for everyone. They made a rookie error and forgot how exhausting travelling is- even if it was only a modest 27 miles. I was shattered- and I didn't even have to do any packing or shift any of the baggage. How grown-ups manage, I just don't know. I was extra tired as the worlds smallest bed was a smidge on the snug side. I needed to be unfolded like a parcel when I woke up as I couldn't even stretch. When you're too big for your bed, it's difficult to get settled. Add to that the midnight blackness of the cabin when the lights went out, strange noises and the gentle ebb and flow of the waves, and everything was a little bit different. And- to her dismay, Mummy forgot my magic music light thing. I don't always want it playing or the stars projected, but on those occasions, it does make a good missile to launch from my crib and onto the unsuspecting floor.

Braced for Mummy karaoke, I tried to feign exhaustion, but the parents could see that I wasn't fully committed to the portrayal of 'tired babe'. A quick google or youtube was out of the question as the Internet was now a forbidden entity on account of it costing a small fortune. And then, Mummy remembered that she had one song downloaded on her phone's library: *Somewhere Over the Rainbow*. Not the Judy Garland gingham and red shoes version. No, one that sounds like a lullaby and was sung by the gentle giant that was Israel Kamakawiwo'ole, an *a capella* version with the Hawaiian singer and his ukulele. Like a moth to a flame, my eyelids began to droop under his dulcet tones and the next thing I knew, I was being awkwardly shoehorned into my compact bed and drifting towards some semblance of sleep.

Every night, *P&O Cruises'* daily newsletter- *Horizon*, is delivered to the post box outside each cabin. By the time Mummy and Daddy retired to bed last night, all they managed was a quick scan of the paper. It's a useful newsletter with an itinerary of events that are happening across the ship, as well as adverts and helpful port information. When I say quick, I mean a 30-second cursory express read, which was enough time to discover that at 10:00 there was a nursery group play session on the theme of Outer Space, down on deck 8. Excellent. This was our destination of choice. With the plans set, we headed to breakfast in a timely manner, arriving at the self-service restaurant up on deck 16 around 09:15. As we walked by the swimming pool beneath the huge retractable dome and giant cinema screen, Mummy's eyebrows did that thing where they give her wrinkles as she glanced at her watch in confusion. Yes, it was still 09:15. So why was the 10:00 screening of *Rio* playing so early? This was very odd, given that the timings on cruise ships run like clockwork. In the end, Mummy guessed that someone had hit the start button a little bit earlier than intended. Instead of pausing the film and waiting until the right time, they just rolled with it and hoped that nobody would notice. But they didn't bank on the musketeers picking up on this projection error! No, Siree.

Shrugging off the strangeness of the film playing at the wrong time, we found a table in the busy restaurant and got me a high chair. Mummy then went to have some milk warmed for my porridge. Things didn't feel quite right. The restaurant was really busy, and yet stations were being closed. When the waiter returned with my porridge milk, Mummy asked him what the time was. He said it was 10:20. Mummy shook her head adamantly. It was 09:20. And then, they had a watch-off. Simultaneously, they both drew their wrists at the same time- the waiter with his digital flashing offering, and Mummy with her analogue battered fake gold and even faker diamond watch. To Mumma's horror, she lost the watch-off and we forfeited an hour. This meant that we musketeers were deprived of a whole sixty minutes as the Time Lords leapt through the time and space continuum whilst we were sleeping. We may well be eligible for timepensation on our return journey though. However, this meant that the 10:00 Outer Space play was now off the table and firmly on the floor.

Leaping an hour into the future before you've even had a bite to eat was highly disconcerting. How did everyone know about the time change? Had we slept through an announcement on the loudspeaker? Were we really that exhausted that none of us heard a thing? No. It transpires that we did not miss an announcement. Instead, at the bottom of the cover page of the *Horizon* newsletter, there was a little note informing us that in the early hours, the clocks on the ship would spring forward an hour. On account of my not being able to yet read words, I believe that I'm absolved from responsibility. With that in mind, I would say to the parents that this incident should serve as a warning as to the dangers of the express read. Cursory scan at your peril.

P&O Cruises also provide a daily newspaper titled *Britain Today*. As you would expect, it's filled with the usual doom and gloom that generally constitutes the newspaper of today. However, there is a tiny box of greatness at the bottom right of the first page. It's called *Today in History* and we decided to cut them out and keep them, because most of the history was a bit more interesting than the current affairs.

TODAY IN HISTORY

On 4th September 1860, the first weather forecast appeared in The Times. In 1909, the first Boy Scout rally took place at Crystal Palace in London. In 1964, the Forth Road Bridge was opened by the Queen.

I wonder what they did before 1860 if there was no weather forecast. Looked out the window perhaps? I may not have been alive and kicking in 1987, but *The Great Storm of '87*, as not predicted by Michael Fish, provided a major dent in the reliability of weather forecasting in my book. Apparently, Mr Fish said that it would be windy in Spain. Perhaps that was accurate. Right now, on our way to Spain, it is in fact rather blustery. I suppose you could take anything from history and turn it into a future prediction. So, Michael Fish may not have been right about the almost-hurricane, but he was certainly correct in foreseeing winds in Spain in 2023.

I'm not really interested in a bridge, even if it is believed to be one of the most significant long-span suspension bridges in the world. Yes, it's a pretty big accolade. But what I'm really interested in is a palace made of crystal. And why is there a football club called Crystal Palace? I don't know a lot of things as I'm still quite new to the world, but I've heard that motto 'people shouldn't throw stones in glass houses'. I imagine you probably shouldn't play football in a palace made of glass either.

Crystal Palace burnt down in 1936, but the club kept the name. I suppose it's a nice way to keep history alive: Crystal Palace FC have the emblem of the palace in their logo. At some point in history, they wandered off-piste and had an unfortunate spell of time where they were known as 'The Glaziers', but common-sense prevailed and they lost the window-fitting connotations. Still, it would have been amazing to see 11,000 scouts at a palace built for a world fair known as the *Great Exhibition of 1851*. At that time, Crystal Palace was the largest building in the whole world, playing host to more than 15,000 exhibitors. It must have been rather impressive.

Fast-forward and back into the present day. What with the original plans as shattered as the palace, our plan B basically involved lots of improvisation and making things up. It was a lot less structured than plan A. As of yet, we've not had to crack open the sun cream. This is disappointing for Mummy as she optimistically packed five bottles.

How's this for daring: today we survived a voyage through the Valley of Death. This is not to be confused with Death Valley in California. No, this Valley of Death is what the sailors of yesteryear affectionately referred to the tumultuous waters of the Bay of Biscay as.

When the parents had their honeymoon in 2016 aboard Azura, they cruised from Southampton and went all the way to Greece. The weather was not very nice and the Bay of Biscay threw up swells between nine and fifteen feet. Or was it metres? Either way, it was very rough and very unfun. For the first three or four days, the outside space and promenade decks were closed to all and sundry. This was Mummy and Daddy's first experience of cruising: being imprisoned on the ship on account of bad weather. For those first few nights, Mummy vividly recalls commandeering the champagne bucket and sleeping with it beside the bed. She even had to crack open the sea sickness tablets. Ironically, she was fine when she was walking around the ship and sitting down for dinner, but as soon as her head touched that pillow, her insides were swilling around like a washing machine on a spin cycle. So naturally, as we approached the Bay of Biscay,

Mummy was filled with trepidation. Fortunately, she needn't have worried on our trip as we emerged unscathed. But this got me thinking, why does such a nice sounding stretch of seaside have such a nefarious reputation?

It turns out that the Atlantic Ocean is to blame for the tempestuous waters of the Bay of Biscay. Biscay itself flanks the western coast of France and the northern coast of Spain. It also borders the Atlantic Ocean, which is a lot deeper than Biscay. This is where the problems arise. The average depth of the Atlantic is 10,951 feet (3,338 m), whereas the average depth of Biscay is 5,725 feet (1,745 m). This creates a bit of a bump and conflicting currents. Factor in the winds from America, as they cross the vast expanse of ocean desert on the way to Europe, they gather in momentum and create swells that become huge breaking waves and that can be felt from as far away as 100 miles from the Bay of Biscay. When they then hit the shallower parts of the Bay- known as the continental shelf, that's when things become a bit perilous and the petulant waters throw a tantrum, so to speak.

Crossing the Bay of Biscay is not for the faint of heart. It appears that there's no particularly good time to sail through it, but if you really have to cross it, between May and August is the most favourable time. September heralds the change in seasons in the Bay as the winds become stormier throughout the autumn and winter months. I feel rather like a swash-buckling pirate, having navigated this stretch of water. But unlike most pirates, I do have both legs in tact, no parrot on my shoulder, no eye patch and definitely no hat, as hats only ever stay on my head for a maximum of two minutes. (And that's a generous two minutes).

There may not have been overly large swells as we passed through Biscay, but the winds could best be described as bracing. They were certainly fresh and strong enough to lift the hair on your head. If anyone had been daring enough to risk a toupee, that would almost certainly have evacuated the head it was warming and fallen unceremoniously into the indigo waters.

While we were waiting for the sun to make an appearance, we completed a lap and a half of the substantial promenade deck that encompasses the entire perimeter of the ship in the breezy weather. At several points, the walkway becomes a bridge that skirts the ships atrium and suspends you directly over the roaring ocean. A poke of the head over the glass and balustrade confirms this and brings the sounds of the wind and sea sharply into focus. I personally didn't look over the edge, but the elongated 'woahhhh's' that both parents uttered was enough to tell me that we were very high up and the sea was very low down.

For the half a lap that would have made two circuits, we zipped indoors. It seems that when you go around the starboard bend at the front of the ship, the walkway there becomes a wind tunnel. The breeze hones in on you like a laser target and tries to knock you off your feet, until you eventually emerge on the port side and the promenade straightens once more. It's almost like you imagined the concentrated gusts.

But the relocation of your eyebrows to the sides of your face would suggest otherwise and gives you away. As quickly as a lightning flash, the winds can change when you're in the middle of nowhere, surrounded by nothing but water that stretches to the furthest reaches of what your eye can see. It's easy to understand why the sailors of the past believed that they were sailing to the end of the world when you're the only vessel on an ocean of infinite depths.

Our final half-lap took us indoors and down a couple of decks to the shopping district. Yes, district. It's a whole area of the ship dedicated to things we don't really need, like watches. Why does anybody require more than one? Unless you're an octopus, I really can't see why you'd need to wear more than one timepiece. There's also jewellery, perfumes, designer clothes, make-up, lotions and potions, fancy gins and alcohol, lego, water bottles, ship memorabilia, water bottles, books, toys, and much more than I can remember. What do all these items have in common? Well, from what I could see, they were all rather pricey. Some of them didn't even have price tags, which is a slippery slope. Daddy once enquired as to how much a fancy hotel would cost for dinner, bed and breakfast. The receptionist turned around and said; if you have to ask, sir, I suggest you can't afford it.' This patronising comment came with a valuable lesson: if there's no price tag, we are not interested.

Honestly, it really does turn out that there's a lot of expensive stuff on these luxury liners that we generally don't need. Sandwich soft toy anyone?

How about a slice of cantaloupe soft toy? Nope, no takers? They're just the tip of a very large iceberg called Merchandiseberg. That said, I was rather taken by the giant octopus, but sadly for me, this was promptly vetoed by Dadnad. Mummy then steered me (literally- I was in the pushchair after all), to a lovely little owl, with a truly exceptional label. I do love a good label and this one was most definitely first class in the land of labels.

Back in the cabin, the parents tried to get me to nap, but I wasn't feeling it. So we had some blustery balcony time instead. Not long later, when I eventually succumbed to sleep in my mini crib, Mummy and Daddy had a picnic lunch and watched an Elvis film.

Later in the day, we went to a *Shaun the Sheep* clay modelling session. You know Shaun— black legs, white fluffy mullet and lives on Mossy Bottom Farm. He's the brainchild of Nick Aardman and landed his own television series in 2007 after making his first appearance in *Wallace and Gromit* in 1995. I didn't know who Shaun was until we were flicking through the television shows and found the entire back catalogue. I understood it right away. As none of the characters speak actual words, all of their actions made perfect sense to me.

The model making took place at three o'clock and said that it was a drop-in session. Our family definition of 'drop-in' is- it turns out, rather different to that of *P&O Cruises*. To us, a drop-in session is looser in its timings. We knew it started at three and finished about three-quarters of an hour later. So, if you're dropping-in, you don't have to be there at three sharp. Instead, you can turn up (like we did) at around twenty-five past, on account of yours truly being asleep at kick-off. And being a drop-in, you can also leave whenever you feel you've dropped enough time into the equation. This is how the ad-hoc nursery that Mummy and I sometimes go to works. But this is not the viewpoint that *P&O Cruises* share. As we took a seat in the practically empty bar lounge in the aft (backside of the boat) you could almost feel the disappointment from the staff at our apparent tardiness. A mat then appeared, some clay and an instruction leaflet, as well as the jolly welcoming information that we'll be finishing in fifteen minutes. Rightoh, we'd best crack on then.

In the advert for the session, it invited you to bring a child along. I was said child, even though I was probably a bit too young for the activity and mistook the modelling clay for an edible delight. I don't know if the staff were a bit annoyed by our interpretation of child, but a glance over our shoulder on the right told us we needn't have worried as there was a couple with their daughter, who must have been about twenty. Children come in all shapes, sizes and ages. She was a senior child and I was the opposite. Anyway, in the non-drop-in space of fifteen minutes, Mummy and Daddy cobbled together a Shaun the sheep as I supervised from my pushchair throne. His eyes were a bit bulgy and his legs a bit lopsided, but that didn't matter because he was *our* sheep and new cabin mascot. Due to his lack of resemblance to actual

Shaun, Mumma and Dadnad nicknamed him Juan- after the great sheep himself, as Juan is Spanish for Shaun. Who knew?!

In the same bar lounge, after the session of Shaun creation had finished, there immediately followed a game of bingo. Lured by the possibility of winning £5,000-00, Mummy and Daddy bought a booklet, believing that when they uttered the immortal words 'BINGO!', their initial £20-00 investment would be recouped. They hadn't decided what they were going to do with the remaining £4,980-00, but I for one know that that can buy a heck of a lot of biscuits, nappies and milk. Anyway, what I am about to divulge is verging on scandalous. Not only did we not win the £5,000-00; we didn't even come close to winning a single game. Worse still, Mummy never got to triumphantly call out 'BINGO!' and wave the ticket enthusiastically in the air. Based on the evidence, I can only assume that we were sold faulty tickets.

The restaurant that we selected for dinner was inordinately busy this evening. It turns out that there's an app where you can book your table. We didn't know about said app, which is a permanent hangover from the pandemic. The people who did know about the app had then block-booked the restaurants that they wanted to visit on the first day. We just thought that they were in need of a WiFi fix before we set sail. But it would appear, they were busy securing their dining for the fortnight.

With no reservation, we were instead provided with a pager that would buzz when a table became available. We were then told that the wait would be at least an hour, but when they saw that I was a bambino, the hour wait suddenly became half of that. So, with thirty minutes to spare, we had a wander and found ourselves at Ocean Studios- Arvia's three screen cinema complex. Two of the three films showing were not baby friendly, but the one in Studio 3 was deemed Brontë suitable. So, we went into the empty cinema and caught the tail-end of Disney's *Encanto*- my first film. Almost. By my own admission, I don't have the attention span to sit through 102 minutes of technicolour delights. But as the cinema was empty, I was free to wander around the space and enjoy the magic of the multi-sensory greatness. It was a feast for my eyes and the music tickled my ears.

To end on a positive note, my mini-bed has been upgraded to a mini-estate bed. It's now the size it's supposed to be. At least I can stretch out and roll over without bouncing off the mesh sides. So in spite of losing an hour, we had a happy sea day, nicely rounded off by a good splash in the tub.

05 September

SILENCIO, POR FAVOR

SUNRISE 08:02
SUNSET 21:00

Hello, happy campers. You'll be pleased to read that I had a much better sleep in my upgraded bed. I woke up feeling refreshed and ready to take on the world. As an added bonus, I even got to have a *Weetabix* on the go as we had room service, because an expedition to the city of Santiago de Compostela beckoned. But before disembarking, let me take you on a trip down memory lane.

28

TODAY IN HISTORY

On 5th September 1666, the Great Fire of
London ends, leaving 13,200 houses
destroyed and 8 dead. In 1997,
Mother Teresa, who was awarded the 1979
Nobel Peace Prize for her charitable work,
died aged 87.

Ninety-eight feet (30 m) beneath Mount Wingen in New South Wales, Australia, there's a fire that has been burning for over 6,000 years. It's known as Burning Mountain. All the best fires in history have a striking name, it seems. There's no Damp Squib Fire of London recorded in history. The name just doesn't conjure up the might of a blazing inferno.

Back to the present day.

P&O Cruises have helpfully included a bit of information about La Coruna (or A Coruña, if we're being Spanish) in the *Horizon* newsletter. Seems as our time spent in La Coruna would be little more than a drive out and a drive back in, it's a useful reference.

WELCOME TO LA CORUNA

The name of La Coruna's cruise dock -
Transatlantic Quay - reflects its location
on the northwestern tip of the Iberian Peninsular
making it - you might be surprised to learn -
the closest European port to New York.

It is a charming mixture of old town and
new town also with a couple of beaches along
the two-mile stretch of coastline it overlooks.
The colonnaded Maria Pita Square is at the
heart of the old town, with many shops, bars
and restaurants all around. There are various
fascinating museums including the interactive
House of Mankind plus an aquarium
and planetarium.

The boat docked at La Coruna early in the morning.
Mummy read somewhere that this area of Spain is
known as the end of the world, which I think you'll
agree is a pretty big proclamation. I don't need to go
to the bottom of Latin America or Antarctica and risk
frost bite, as I can now confidently say that I've been
to the end of the world. What's more, I'm only on day
three of my holiday. What a result.

The Roman's gave this rugged headland the name
Finisterre, which is Latin and literally translates
as 'end of the Earth'. Historically speaking, this is a
significant place as this was the area for one's final
port of call before sailing into the unknown realms
of the Atlantic Ocean. Or, as the Spanish say, Océano
Atlantico. Mummy also heard that La Coruna is where
the Spanish Armada bid adios from, before sailing
for England's shores in 1588, but that is wrong. The
Spanish Armada- ironically, set sail in May of the same
year from Lisbon, which by my calculations is actually
in a different country called Portugal. Although, from
1580 and for the next sixty years, Portugal was under

Spanish rule. Who knew? No wonder Mummy's brain cells got all jumbled up as she had operated under the knowledge that Spain's greatest naval defeat and the inspiration behind Elizabeth I's 'Heart of a Lion' speech, were connected to Finisterre. Not so.

In the interests of clarity, in 1589, in retaliation for the Spanish sending what was- at the time, the largest naval gathering of some 150 ships and about 18,000 men, the English launched a revenge attack, now known as the Siege of Coruna. It ended in failure a fortnight later and the English trudged up to Lisbon instead. Still, everyone seems to be friends now and Anglo-Spanish relations appear to be quite bonny.

When we disembarked Arvia, we walked along the side of the ship as we headed to our tour guide and coach. Gee whizz, she's a beast of machinery. If you can believe it, the boat is bigger than our whole house! That's because it can hold 5,200 guests and 1,800 crew. Which is about 6,994 more than our house likes to accommodate in any one sitting.

A couple of Arvia facts for you.

She entered service in 2022 and weighs in at 184,700 tonnes. I, on the other hand, also entered service in 2022, but I did not weigh quite so much. At my inaugural weigh-in on 05 May, I topped the scales at 6 lb 11 oz.

We've got our cabin in the Forward section, a couple of decks lower than the captain and his crew and their giant steering wheel. Mummy's seen *Pirates of the Caribbean*, so she knows exactly what she's talking about and how the ship is steered. They may even store the plank up on the Bridge. Anyway, being at the front of the ship means that it can be a bit wibbly-wobbly in the cabin when there's any strong winds or currents. That said, it is very exciting to be able to see your direction of travel without having to crane your neck at an awkward angle.

Arvia parked- or docked, if we're being technical.

Our cabin is on the port side. To non-mariners, port is the left and starboard is the right. Our cabin is 12110, with the 12 indicating the deck and the 110 the room. On the port side you have the even cabins and the odd numbers on the starboard side. For prosperity, I stuck a picture of Arvia into my journal, taken from the port side (and gratefully extracted from a brochure procured from the on-board sales area. Thank you *P&O Cruises*). However, the image that you can see is one that Mumma took of Arvia. The parents got quite excited that they could see our cabin when viewing Arvia from this angle. It made them feel 'muy importante' and me, most important.

Sorry, I have digressed. Back to the business of our expedition to Santiago de Compostela. We found our coach and our pregnant tour guide. I think she was called Sabela. (She said her name was Galician, which is this region of Spain). We hopped on the coach at La Coruna, immediately leaving the sunshine behind in the port. This was disappointing, so in protest, I gave an almighty wail as the coach left. From our back seat, I could almost see the shoulders slump of all the other guests en masse on our tour as my lungs roared into action. But it was okay- I was mourning the loss of the sunshine. As quick as a flash, Mummy delved into the trusty treat tub as I sat on Daddy's lap. She gave me a white chocolate bribe, sorry- white chocolate button, which I clung to for dear life until it started to melt. Ah, what a glorious moment that was.

Following a swift and efficient clean-up operation after the button melting episode, I then made sure that my nap buddy had a firm hold of me. With two large Daddy hands around my waist, I made the executive decision to use my time wisely and have a snooze. My nap buddy also decided to rest his eyes as the gentle hum of the coach engine lulled us into Napland. My nap buddy really is the best that there is.

An observation from the coach: the region of Galicia is very green. It could easily be confused with France or Scotland, just by looking at the trees and valleys. As Mummy was thinking this, the tour guide then explained that Northern Spain is typically a lot greener than the rest of Spain. She also informed us that we could easily expect four seasons in one day. Thanks to my Vivaldi music book that I have with me in the cabin, I already do. Luckily, Mummy was a Brownie and insisted on packing our waterproofs in our excursion bag. Nana said that we wouldn't need our coats on holiday, but Mummy is far too sensible to leave home without them. My nappy bag goes everywhere I go and features everything you could possibly require for a day out. Generally speaking, we use about 10% of what we actually bring with us. But as Daddy the former boy scout likes to remind Mummy, Robert Baden-Powell-the founder of the scouts, encouraged us all to BE PREPARED. And that was back in 1908. So prepared we are.

Let's use the tour guide's name (or what I think her name is) as it feels a bit more friendly. Sabela told us that Galicia is a Celtic nation (within Spain) and that the national instrument of the region is the bagpipes. Yes, really! Sure enough, as we were walking to the cathedral from the drop-off, there was a man expertly playing the bagpipes. It was a beautiful- and yet, haunting, melancholy tune.

One of the tours offered by *P&O Cruises* from La Coruna was to see a lighthouse. We considered this option before electing to go to Santiago de Compostela- the final destination at the end of the oldest pilgrimage in Europe. Annually, over 300,000 pilgrims make the journey and around 4 million tourists visit the city. For a city with a population of roughly 96,000, these are big numbers. So intrigue and an hour or so's journey time trumped a visit to the oldest working lighthouse in the world. We drove by it and saw it in the distance. It was a smidge underwhelming. Considering it's a rather famous lighthouse, I was disappointed to find that it wasn't painted red and white, as all good lighthouses are. Perhaps they didn't have those colours of paint in the Roman era? Or was it the Medieval era? I was asleep, so am unable to verify Mummy's memory. But I think Sabela said Roman, or possibly Romanesco. No, wait. That's lettuce. We're getting off topic here.

A retrospective bit of research informs me that it is in fact a lighthouse of Roman origins, more commonly referred to as the Tower of Hercules (Torre de Hercules) because Hercules was flexing his muscles and doing a spot of freelance hero-work. Rumour has it that in honour of Hercules burying the head of a slain monster beneath the lighthouse, he had the building named after him. You can actually walk the 242 steps to the top of the building, but this would not have been toddler compatible.

Speaking of walking, to be an official pilgrim of Santiago de Compostela, you've got to walk at least 62 miles (100 km) or cycle over 124 miles (200 km). To do this, you must have to really love Jesus, the fresh air, and walking- or a spot of all three. It seems that a lot of people do, as in 2022, over 440,000 people made the pilgrimage. On the day we've gone, as many as 2,000 tourists might stop by, including us.

I have included a sketch photo of the cathedral as it is so big that it is almost impossible to take a selfie without losing the tops of this extraordinary building. Every photo that Mummy and Daddy tried to take had lots of tourists and visitors in the way. That said, they did manage to get a picture of the three of us in front of the cathedral looking exceptionally windswept and verging on bedraggled. It seemed rather pointless to include said image though as I am in a parent-sandwich, squished unceremoniously in between them with a grimace on my face and half of the cathedral behind us. In our defence, we were in classic tourist mode and had to get the requisite giant cathedral snap, at the detriment of a smile.

The mighty Santiago de Compostela, complete with just a handful of tourists as it was quite early.

Abandoning any further photography opportunities, we then had a whistle-stop explore of the cathedral as I was feeling a bit ratty and ended up enjoying the cathedral acoustics a bit too much. A Spanish lady over a tannoy kept saying '¡Silencio, por favor!' I'm fairly certain that she was talking exclusively to me as nobody else was experimenting with the echo, apart from yours truly- the trail-blazing toddler. Still, I knew to be quiet when Mummy and Daddy lit a candle for someone very special- Gracie, who I never got the chance to meet but is a big bright star in the sky upstairs. I then had my milk by the confession box and in front of a big statue of the Virgin Mary. Once fully refreshed, we left the cathedral and the lady desperate for silence. On our way towards the exit, we found a dime all the way from America and left the cathedral richer than when we first went in. It's not a marketing ploy- people really do come from all over the world to visit this cathedral. I put the dime into my journal for safekeeping. It's worth 10 cents. You never know, what with inflation, by the time I'm an adult, that $0.10 might have gone up to a dollar or ten.

Outside the cathedral, there were literally hundreds of tourists and pilgrims of all ages. The pilgrims looked both exhausted and exhilarated in equal measure. Interestingly, the pilgrims weren't all people of the older persuasion. There was a whole array of ages on display and lots of people in their twenties.

We had lunch in the square, following a walk-about-wonder. The parents chose regional delicacies and

Spanish staples: a coffee, a Galician beer, 'pulpo' aka octopus and 'empanada', which is a type of Spanish pie. I didn't risk the octopus, but Mummy and Daddy did and they both lived to tell the tale, which is a relief. I did, however, try the empanada. It's essentially a pie with any ingredients they can find but don't disclose. It's the Russian roulette of the Spanish culinary world. I rounded my meal off with some complimentary *P&O Cruises* breakfast yoghurt and fruit.

On the return journey, I once again slept with my nap buddy. Being a sightsee-er is more tiring than I realised. Later, we ended up abandoning our dinner plans on account of the overstimulation that was the dining area. There were simply too many people and far too much noise that made us all feel a bit stressed and not relaxed. So, we returned to the cabin and I had magic milk before bed.

IT'S A
PIRATES LIFE FOR ME
M'HEARTIES!

06 September

SEARCH WARRANT FOR SEÑOR SUNSHINE

SUNRISE 08:13
SUNSET 20:57

The third in command has just this morning announced two things over the tannoy: 1). that he is the third in command and evidently feels that this is vital information for the guests, and 2). that it's currently 13 degrees Celsius. That's a wee bit fresh for holiday weather in my book. Like most people, I tend to think that a holiday involves feeling the sun warming your skin. Even if you went on a skiing trip, you'd still be wearing the UV goggles on account of the strength of the sun. So it really wasn't too much to expect the sun to come out and put his hat on, hip hip hooray. It appeared- however, that he had other ideas and was content to loiter back home and toast the UK with a final summer heatwave before heading south and crossing the Equator for a stint of summer business. Still, we know that both parents are the BE PREPARED sort, so with the BE PREPARED genes running through my veins, I made sure that I had an adequate supply of leggings. They were there on a contingency basis for instances when the sun had absconded from the sky- just like today.

Not only is it cooler than anticipated, it's also a bit windier than planned. The sun taking a leave of absence doesn't really bother me that much. I can handle that. What I'm finding a bit more of a challenge is mastering the sway of the boat, due to the wind. As a novice walker (and by novice, I mean about twelve days into the vertical operation), the perpetual motion makes it more difficult to find my centre of gravity, meaning that I am liable to topple over in any direction at any given moment. I've not yet found my sea legs. I'm sure people must think that I'm milk drunk!

We had a very nice, tranquil breakfast this morning up at the self-service buffet. It turns out that 08:20 is not a popular time for holidaymakers on a cruise ship. The only people that were there were members of- what Daddy calls, 'The Early Morning Club'. Mummy disagrees and thinks that they're members of a rival faction known as 'The Society for Peace and Quiet'. Me? Well, I just think that they were hungry and decided that because they were awake, they'd have their breakfast and get the day started. I base this conclusion on my own personal experience.

A bit later, Mum and Dadnad took me to a baby group at 10:00 called 'Turtle Tots'. They met in The Club House on deck 8, which was where we would have gone if we hadn't have lost the hour. The gathering that we missed was outer space themed, but today's was pirates.

The girls running the pirate play class distributed bandanas to all of the assembled babes to help us get into character and embrace the mood of the skull and cross bones flag waving brigade. Mummy took it out of politeness. She knew that it would be fruitless to even try to attempt to conceal my curls beneath a bandana. My headwear rule is simple: unless it's my hair and attached to my scalp, my head is not an ornamental decorative stand under any circumstances. The day before we went on holiday, Nana and I went through my zoo book and I demonstrated the noise that a lion makes. If tested, I can roar. And just like any good lion, I am protective of my mane. So, Mummy instead offered me the black fabric as a sort of handkerchief to wave. I looked at her blankly and thought that because she seemed to be enjoying the bandana flag so much, I would leave her to it. Why deprive her of an activity that brings so much joy?

Parents don't need much to be happy- just some of life's simple pleasures really. And a lot of life's simple pleasures can be found in nursery groups or activities aimed at children. Generally, the children aren't overly interested in the fun that's been planned for them. It's the parents that then end up doing the activity and having the fun, whilst the child riffles through the Mummy's handbag and searches for contraband in there instead. Because we all know that some rules are made to be broken. If Mummy's didn't want their offspring to explore their handbags, they should simply put them out of arms reach and firmly lock them with a padlock. Otherwise, they're just inviting tiny hands to go rummaging.

The pirate shenanigans went on for about twenty minutes. If truth be told, I lost interest quite quickly and wondered off in the opposite direction when the other babes went off on a pseudo treasure hunt, trudging along behind a lady with a wannabe ventriloquist parrot on her shoulder. Mummy says I'm a non-conformist. Daddy agrees. I'm not quite sure what that is, but I for one certainly don't like to follow the crowd. So I didn't.

Having walked the plank and jumped ship, we returned to cabin ahoy!, and I had my milk followed by a good, hearty nap. It was exactly what the captain ordered.

TODAY IN HISTORY

On September 6th, 1879, the first British telephone exchange opened in Lombard Street, London. In 1990, cricketer Sir Len Hutton, the first professional to captain England, died aged 74.

I found the historical events a bit underwhelming today. I don't know anything about the England cricket captain. I also don't know anything about cricket, so it makes sense that I haven't the foggiest clue who Sir Hutton is, or was. Likewise, I don't know what a telephone exchange is, but I do know that most exchanges became obsolete in the 1960's due to automation, but some stubbornly clung on until the eighties. Still, having always known the telephone my whole life, it must have been an extraordinary moment- tantamount to divine intervention, to the first person who dialled a number, was picked up by a telephonist and put through to the intended recipient, as if by magic.

After I woke up from my nap, Mummy said I looked cute and went to fetch the instant polaroid camera that makes all the pictures look like they were taken in the seventies and eighties (it's retro). In my efforts to help push the button, which, incidentally I am very good at (this is a newly acquired skill and one that I am justly proud of), my hand leapt into my portrait like an unexpected alien. But that's the beauty of instant pictures that you can't edit or tweak: you never know what you're going to get. It's pot luck.

After sharing with you my thoughts on *P&O Cruises* merchandise and wares in the shopping district yesterday, I'm sorry to say that I succumbed to the lure of the little wise owl. After all, the owl is the icon of my favourite Greek goddess- Athena, so it's no surprise that I have an affinity with these creatures.

For £10-00, I was able to adopt my new owl. As a surprise, Nana gave me this money to spend on our holiday. So I spent it wisely. Although, probably not quite as wisely as my great-great-uncle on Mummy's side and my great-uncle on Daddy's side, who both spent their respective £10-00 on a passage to Australia back in the 1960's when the telephone exchange was on borrowed time. £10-00 was all it cost to start a new life Down Under and was used to cover the cost of the processing fees involved in migrating from the UK to Australia. In early 2022, Mummy's brother, my uncle, also decided to emigrate to Australia. But I'm fairly certain that he paid a lot more than £10-00 to do it.

My new owl is very sweet. She's a tawny and quite small- no more than seven or eight inches tall. She's lucky that I rescued her from a life spent in a gift shop, where she would be perpetually waiting to be freed from shelf-servitude and a life on the seven seas. With my Nana present, I was able to gift my owl with a new life with me and my stuffed animal friends including Little Chick, Charlie Chick, Lamb Chop, Buddy Bear and Tabbit the Rabbit. They're really great pals of mine- especially Little Chick. I've only lost Little Chick once (we don't include the time he vanished for two and a half weeks, only to be found under my cot-bed. That was just an extended game of Hide and Seek). No, he's only been lost outside of the house on one occasion. When Mummy realised that Little Chick was nowhere to be seen, she filed a missing person's report with the relevant powers that be. When asked for any distinguishing features, she replied that 'he's about six inches tall and bright yellow'.

To my utter delight, some civically minded member of the public handed Little Chick in and a week later, I was happily reunited with him. Since then, I have become a much more careful and attentive owner. That said, I will often voluntarily launch Little Chick from my cot and send him skywards. So fair warning to Henrietta, my newly christened owl: I might accidentally drop you on your head, but I will love you as much as a sixteen month old can.

As with yesterday, I had a play in the nursery to burn off some energy. I particularly enjoyed the soft play equipment and being able to launch myself blindly, knowing that Mummy and Daddy will be there to catch me and prevent any maritime disasters. My job as a Professional Toddler is to keep the parents on their toes, something I endeavour to do to the best of my ability.

We completed a bracing walk up on deck 18. This is where the infinity pool is and splash zone for young children, as well as giant chess and the steps up to the crazy golf and high ropes course on deck 19- Arvia's top deck. There's also a mini promenade that they call a jogging circuit. Although they didn't jog, Mumma and Naddad did embark on a brisk walk that was just a hop, skip and a jump away from being a jog, due to the wind chill of the icy breeze. We did seven laps, which equated to a mile. It was very foggy and I think I actually tasted cloud- a very surreal moment in my day.

Tonight it was Black Tie. This meant that formal dress was a requirement for the majority of the eateries. However, Daddy had had a premonition involving me, flying foods, and subsequent disasters featuring said food landing in a bowl of blood red tomato soup and splashing all over the white jacket of a moustachioed waiter, like a scene from a horror film. Fearful that his premonition would become a reality, an executive decision was made: there would be no formal nights for us. We did still dress up for the occasion though, which was nice- even if we were only going to the self-service restaurant. And do you know what we found? Ice cream. Of the chocolate variety. After dinner, I tried one perfectly round ball that resembled a muddy puddle by the time I got to it. Truly, it was scrumptious. And even better, it made me look like I was wearing lipstick.

With seas that appeared to calm as the evening progressed, I was able to walk the length of the corridor from the lifts in the forward, all the way to our accommodation. They say that a lot can change in a day. I say that a lot can change in a few hours. This morning I was a stumbling stepper. This evening, I am pleased to report that I am now a walker and growing in confidence with every passing minute.

THE HAIR ELIXIR

07 September

CALL OFF THE SEARCH- THE SUN HAS BEEN FOUND

SUNRISE UNKNOWN- SOMETIME
IN THE MORNING AFTER THE DAWN
SUNSET UNKNOWN- SOMETIME
IN THE EVENING AFTER DUSK*

* My apologies, dear Reader, but it appears that the piece of the newsletter with the sunrise and sunset times has absconded. By which I mean that either I ripped this portion of the paper out whilst practicing my motor skills. Or, Mummy tore it out to stick into my journal because she was more interested in what was on the other side. It can't have been Daddy because he wouldn't be daring enough to tear such vital information away. However, in this instance, seems as Mummy is old enough to know better, let's say that the times are missing because Mummy was having a maverick five minutes. This is perfectly plausible, by the way. In an act of wilful rebellion, Mummy once removed a picture of Lake Annecy (France), from the magazine in a hotel bedroom. This was before I was on the scene and offered page removal services to rival that of Mum's. In her defence, she needed it to help write a book as the azure waters of the lake, flanked by the mountains and commanded by a beautiful white hotel called the Impérial Palace, formed a pivotal location in the world that she was creating. That world is called *The Upstairs*.

Hurrah! Following on from my walking progress, I have at long last found my sea legs. They appeared sometime after we traversed the busy shipping lane that is the Gibraltar Strait. Today, we were one of roughly 300 ships that would have sailed through these waters. Annually, about 60,000 boats of all shapes and sizes pass through the 8 mile (13 km) wide strait. We snuck through around 6 am this morning, so- strictly speaking, I was asleep. But, when I woke up, my legs were ready for walking and boy have I walked today!

Now that I'm a walker, I don't want to have my newly found freedom curtailed. Because, from what I've seen, as soon as babes have learnt to walk, the Mummy's and Daddy's are telling them not to and trying to stop them from exploring. Parents really do worry too much. Still, whenever I've been in those infernal high chairs for too long, I am desperate to stretch my legs and attempt a few doddery steps that- if I'm lucky, will break out from a trot and into a canter. Honestly, when was the last time you were strapped into a wooden contraption without any cushions? You'd be wanting to walk if you were in my shoes. You see, I've tasted freedom and it is mighty fine. With every passing day, I'm feeling more and more like Bruce Springsteen. Because baby, I was born to run. Parents, I give you fair warning.

Confession time: I'm absolutely zonked. As excited as I am to be able to move myself sort-of independently from A to B, it is tiring. In proportion to me and in relation to my size, I've probably walked a mini marathon. I now realise I was foolhardy in my thoughts and retract my diary entry from the third of September. Sleep, it turns out, is not for losers after all. It's for winners and winners need to recharge their batteries. Tomorrow, we've got a busy day in Valencia, so I need to be on top form.

TODAY IN HISTORY

On Sep 7, 1533, Queen Elizabeth I was born at Greenwich Palace in London, the first born daughter of Henry VIII and Anne Boleyn. In 1901, the Peace of Peking ended the Boxer Rising in China.

Tudor history seems to be popular at the moment. Elizabeth I is one of the greats, in my opinion. In British history, she is on the podium of super long ruling lady monarchs. Behind Queen Elizabeth II and

Queen Victoria, Queen Elizabeth I reigned for the third longest time of the ladies, putting in a good stint with 44 years and 127 days. She started her rule in 1558 and retired on account of being dead in 1603. Long before the Spice Girls were on the scene, she was the original beholder of Girl Power. Plus, her Mum was Mummy's favourite wife of Henry VIII. And because Anne Boleyn is Mummy's favourite, by default she's my favourite. Plus, Anne Boleyn had the best headwear of the six, so that puts her heads and shoulders above the other wife contestants. (Excuse the perfectly timed pun. It had to be done).

Back to the present. Today was quite relaxed. The sun decided to make an appearance, so we took full advantage of that. Beforehand, we had some breakfast, booked a trip for one of our two days in Barcelona and then booked Mummy in for a spa appointment to fix her hair. I didn't know her hair was broken, but she says that it's been a bit frizzy since having babies. So, she booked a de-frizzing session- or something like that, for later in the afternoon. I'm not sure what happened when Mummy was in the salon, but I'm reliably informed that she had to sit in a recliner chair, place her head in a sink (still attached. Not like Anne Boleyn), had various potions slathered on, and then a blow dry and straighten.

I was hanging out with Daddy when Mummy came to meet us back in the cabin. She looked very glamorous for a lady wearing dungarees and her hair was shiny and smooth. I couldn't communicate this information, so I just beamed at her and thought that that would suffice. She then tried to discreetly hide a fancy bag, but nothing gets past Mrs Bongles. I swiftly intervened and extracted a fancy shampoo and conditioner. Yes, Mummy had fallen prey to the up-sale. It was only after the hairdresser had finished coiffing Mummy's bouffant that he told her that if she wanted the results to last for the full six weeks, she would require the special potions that he'd used. Daddy shook his head in what I imagine must have been polite incredulity. But, if we reframe our thoughts on the accidental purchase of the eye-wateringly expensive hair products, they were a gift from *P&O Cruises* to Mummy, as they were purchased with our on-board credit. Thus, they were free. That, my friends, is called deductive reasoning. Not bad for a one year old.

We watched a *Wallace and Gromit* show in the outdoor venue- the Skydome, with lots of other passengers. It was quite good- albeit very loud. I liked the music. And if truth be told, I hadn't realised how much I'd missed hearing it. At home, we listen to music all the time. When I was *in utero*, Mummy was a busy piano teacher and had over thirty students. I used to listen to their efforts all day long and can tell you that some were better than others. I used to give Mum's tum a big clout if they were especially bad. And if they were good, I liked to gently kick along in time. Such fond memories. Music is definitely in my soul and makes me very happy. The characters on stage held my attention when there was music. They tried to keep me engaged when they were acting and talking, but sadly they lost out to the fascinating artificial foliage around the poolside stage. By my own admission, my attention span can be quite limited and prone to disperse to the more interesting distractions. Like pretend plants. Or anyone with biscuits.

Towards the end of the show, Gromit appeared and then, dressed as a captain, Wallace turned up to wave. It did make me smile to see Captain Gromit on stage, because he was a giant dog and even taller than Daddy! He did doggy dancing, which I enjoyed. I was less enamoured by Captain Wallace, but I did think that the idea of a cruise ship on legs was quite sensible because it could walk on land and queue jump. It's certainly an idea with legs. And speaking of legs, we used ours to walk two circuits of the promenade deck before abandoning all hope, all ye who enter the wild winds of the ocean. It was certainly bracing.

Maramis, d'Adtaganan and I changed into our swimming gear and headed to play in the Splash Zone. Yes, it was blowing a hooley, but that didn't matter. Why didn't it matter, I hear you ask? Well, dear Reader, we were on holiday. And when you are on holiday, you grit your teeth (if you have them. I've only got six at the last count), and you embrace the super fresh water with a smile and grimace. Why? Because you're on holiday, darn it. And you will enjoy yourself, darn it. So, we ignored the goosebumps and tentatively stepped into the puddly Splash Zone. Holy mackerel. What a freeze fest. I'm still defrosting as I write this. Honestly, the water was so cold that I started shivering. And when the water cascaded down the giant metal palm trees or leapt skywards out of the sprinklers, when the wind caught it, it was like being in a hail storm in your pants.

Hastily, we abandoned the splashy play space and slipped into the infinity pool on deck 18. What an experience it was to swim in a pool, when on top of the ocean! It was lots of fun and I got to do a plentiful amount of splashing and pretend to channel my inner mermaid. As a Taurus, my zodiac sign may well be an earth dweller. But once I'm in water, I'm an honorary Piscean, just like Daddy. The symbol for Pisces is two fish that are swimming in opposite directions, whilst tied together by a rope. That's me and Dadnad: a real Pisces and one that's jumped onto the bandwagon and is clinging on to the legitimate one for dear life. That's actually quite accurate as when in the water, I cannot yet swim unaided and require parental assistance at all times.

All in all, it's been a jolly good day, rounded off by a magnificent bath. Mummy brought my hair-wash jug and I've been practicing pouring water out of it, now that I am strong enough to hold and tip it. I was also enjoying the company of my four favourite bath companions: Mr Whale (a whale), Nemo (a fish), Squirt (a turtle) and Crabowski (a crab). I do like a good splash during bath time. And as there's only space in the petite bathroom for one parent to supervise, I like to see how far my splashes can reach. Mummy grabbed a towel and wrapped it around herself and newly slicked locks, leaving just a face. I think she took inspiration from Sister Julienne and her cohorts in *Call the Midwife*. Once she was adequately protected from the Brontë elements, she was very praiseworthy of my splashing skills.

For prosperity, I am recording here in my journal that my seven postcards (purchased from a street vendor within the orbit of Santiago de Compostela) were sent today. We paid £16-10 for the postage at the Reception and were told that they'd be leaving the ship tomorrow, when we're in port. It'll be interesting to see how long it takes for them to reach everyone. Mummy's still waiting for a postcard sent to her from fifteen years ago.

I'M AS TALL AS A PENGUIN!!

08 September

GONE FISHING

SUNRISE 07:39
SUNSET 20:17

Room service beckoned this morning, followed by an early exit from the boat and an independent excursion to Spain's third largest city and one-time capital. Today, Valencia (València in Español) welcomed us to her shores. During the tumult of the Spanish Civil War (1936 - 1939), Valencia had the honour of being the nation's capital for eleven months. The temporary relocation was made so that Madrid would be protected from the Francoists and any potential attacks by them. To clear up a bit of confusion in our heads, Barcelona is not the Spanish capital- even if Mumma had a moment of Mummy Brain and thought that it *was* the capital. She had the tune of Freddie Mercury and Montserrat Caballé's Barcelona song reverberating around her mind. That was written for the 1992 Summer Olympic Games, hosted by Barcelona. Awkwardly for Madrid, the *actual* Spanish capital city, there are a lot less songs written about them than Barcelona, and they have never hosted the Olympics. They've tried- unsuccessfully, to bid to host the games, on three separate occasions. They've always been met with the same answer: 'no, señor y señora'. So why did Mumma think that Barcelona was the capital? Well, it turns out that Barcelona is actually Spain's second biggest city, in between Madrid and Valencia. Barcelona is also the Catalan capital, so that's probably the source of confusion. Mummy's brain put two and two together and came up with fifty-seven.

The weather is always important to us British- perhaps on account of its variability and notorious unreliability back home. Valencia was scorchio and got to about 27 degrees Celsius, which is roughly double the temperature of what I'm used to. Although, this must seem positively balmy compared to when the mercury hit 46.8 degrees Celsius just last month on the 12 August. I don't think I'd have been able to cope with that level of heat. Come to think of it, I don't think Mummy and Daddy would have fared very well either. As it was, on account of the toasty warmth, we had to seek shelter in the air conditioned spaces of L'Oceanogràfic- the largest aquarium in Europe. It also happens to be one of the largest aquariums in the world and is beaten in size only by China and Singapore. The aquarium is home to 500 species of 45,000 animals. Annually, some 2 million visitors are expected to pass through the doors. Even though our trip to the aquarium meant sacrificing a day of sightseeing around the city, it was totally worth it. I doubt the air conditioning would have been quite as good anywhere else as it was in the deliciously polar 'Arctic Zone'. The thing was, once we'd stepped foot into the Arctic, I cooled off a little too well and ended up dozing off. Twice. This entry should really read something more like this...

Dear Diary,

Today we went to the aquarium. There was an amazing beluga whale that swam right up to us and was probably appealing for help to be released as beluga's can live in packs of a thousand and this one was swimming on her lonesome. Only, I wouldn't have known this because I missed her powering through the water on account of being asleep. As such, I was unable to confer with the beluga and translate for Mummy and Daddy. I did wake up though, before we left the Arctic exhibit, and can confirm that I did see the beluga. She was indeed jaw-droppingly awesome.

Over and out,
Explorer Bongles

To get to the aquarium, we had to board the shuttle bus out of the port. Even though we were passing through a shipping area to reach the city, it was very picturesque. The roads were huge- at one point, there was a section of the road with seven lanes of traffic- for one direction! This volume of traffic sent shivers down Mummy's spine. She doesn't mind driving, but if we lived somewhere like Valencia, she'd probably hide her driving licence to avoid having to run the gauntlet of multiple lanes of cars, filled with drivers impatient to reach their destination. Driving, it seems, is no longer a leisurely pursuit.

The shuttle service stopped outside the 1.2 mile (2 km) long Ciutat de les Arts i les Ciències (that's the City of Arts and Sciences to the likes of you and I). From there, a fifteen minute walk would lead you to the Old Town, but we didn't have time to contemplate stepping into the past as the structures of the third millennium awaited our attention.

As we stepped off the shuttle, it was like witnessing a land out of the future, as imagined by those back in the 1950s. Everything was so clean, efficient and aesthetically pleasing. As Daddy likes his architecture, it blew his mind to know that the first area (the Hemisfèric) of this mini city was opened pre-millennium in 1998. Under the watchful eye of the architects Santiago Calatrava and Félix Candela, the Ciutat de les Arts i les Ciències rose from the old (now dried up) river bed of the River Turia like a phoenix and was reincarnated in a pseudo-futuristic incarnation.

There are six areas that make up the City of Arts and Sciences. They are: the València Opera House (and performing arts centre), the Hemisfèric (a laserium, planetarium and IMAX cinema in a building shaped like an eye), the Prince Felipe Museum of Science (in a building inspired by a whale skeleton), the Oceanogràfic (aquarium with an emblem of a water lily- not to be confused with a crown or sharks teeth), the Agora (the newest building and a multi-purpose venue. It reminded us of a gargantuan blue whale swimming vertically toward the surface), and the Umbracle (a landscaped park garden covering about 3280 square feet (1000 m^2) beneath a sizeable lattice roof).

From left to right, the Hemisfèric is in the foreground, followed by the Prince Felipe Museum of Science and then the Agora. To the right is the walkway running parallel and beneath the Umbracle.

The Umbracle is where we hopped off the shuttle. Loosely translated, it means 'the shade' or, from Catalan to English; the umbrella. It's a mighty rectangular structure that flanks one side of the mini city and that the traffic skirts around. The construction is raised above the road level as it conceals a car park, so we walked alongside it on our way to the aquarium. We took a few pictures as we sauntered along, but we were so shiny on account of the heat that we were practically reflective. However, once we'd visited the aquarium and were heading back to the shuttle, we detoured via this 1049 feet (320 m) long oasis, marvelling at the many different varieties of Mediterranean plants that were flourishing. It felt rather surreal, after having first walked alongside the pristine turquoise waters that embrace the Cituat de les Arts i les Ciències.

At ground level of the Umbracle there are multiple indigo mosaic-tiled recesses. I'm being as polite as I can here. One lady on our bus described them as looking like giant urinals. Unfortunately, once seen, that cannot be unseen, for these gently curving recesses did indeed look like urinals on steroids. Of course, the urinal description does not feature anywhere on any of the sanctioned literature, but it does beg the question- when these were being designed and subsequently constructed, did nobody *really* not notice what they resembled?

Urinals aside, when I'm a bit bigger, I'd like to come back here and explore. As soon as you enter this avant-garde space, it's like the time outside of that bubble stops and you're in a different world. It was marvellous.

Back in the aquarium, after we'd bid adios to the beluga and glorious air conditioning, we continued through to the next exhibit- the Antarctic Zone, whose star attraction were the penguins. They also had some ice at the end of the wall which you could touch to see how cold it was. If you're wondering, the answer is very cold. The penguins were all rather jolly, although they were a lot smaller than I imagined. David Attenborough and his cronies have a lot to answer for. When you see penguins in their natural habitat in huge, sprawling groups across acres of icy and rocky areas, they look very big- like Daddy sized. But I guess, there's no point of reference to have a comparable for the true height. Fortunately, the clever aquarium designers thought this through and provided an area of shallow tiered seating from which to survey the penguins.

On the wall, the aquarium team had helpfully put up a scaled picture of every species of penguin in ascending order from smallest to largest. It turns out that there are seventeen different penguin varieties in the world. I know, that's impressive stuff, but prepare to be blown away and even more impressed: I am taller than sixteen of the seventeen penguin species and I'm only sixteen months. The only penguins that were bigger than me were the Emperor penguins. They are known as the giants of the penguin world and can reach the dizzying heights of almost 4 feet (120 cm). And, as if it isn't mind-blowing enough to discover that I am actually penguin sized, did you know that they are birds? But- like me, they can't fly either. How do I know this? Because we've all tried and failed epicly.

Another *Did You Know?*, coming at you. Did you know that a blue whale can grow to 30 metres long? In old school, that's just shy of 100 feet and about the size of two buses, nose to tail, and stuck together. My brain can't even begin to comprehend an animal of that scale.

I'm not sure how science boffs know this, but it's estimated that five or six fully grown human adults could comfortably sit in the space of a whale's heart chambers. And- I don't know if this is true, or if it has ever been substantiated, but an adult could swim through a blue whale's arteries, because they are that large.

We watched the dolphin show in a big open-air stadium with raised seats in a semi-circle amphitheatre configuration around one side. It was mostly in Spanish, so I didn't really follow much of the commentary. But occasionally, the hostess dipped into English, which was helpful. It was also rather hot, so I stripped down to my vest. This was my first real live theatre event, which is noteworthy in itself. However, the thing was, my tummy was rather empty and in need of replenishment. So, on account of using my concentration reserves up on trying to eat in a confined space without losing my nourishment, I was unable to adequately multi-task and fully focus on the dolphin acrobatics.

If it's any consolation, the blueberry muffin that had been liberated from the room service tray was totally worth it. Ask me again in a few years time and I might feel differently, but that muffin was magnificent and worthy of ones full and undivided attention. I did see the dolphins, but I'm fickle you see. Much like the performing dolphins who were rewarded with edible treats, us bambinos can be easily bought for the price of one muffin, one carrot cracker, some fruit, and a bottle of milk.

Next up, we took the lift down to a subterranean level to see the sharks. This was a very popular exhibit with an iconic underwater tunnel. We didn't loiter too long in this area as it was loud and busy, with people seeking the chill of the air conditioning and the thrill of the sharks and all their teeth. That said, a stingray did swim over my head and smiled, which was rather memorable for Mummy- Daddy was holding me and we were looking at Mummy as she took our picture, so we missed the smiling happy stingray.

We saw the crocodiles basking in the sun. They really do look like a relic of the pre-historic era. We watched flamingoes doing what flamingoes do, saw sea-lions, turtles, giant tortoises, seals, tropical fish, jelly fish, and lots of exotic plants. The one place we didn't venture into was the Wetlands/ Aviary as the queues were lengthy and it involved stepping into a huge circular cage and into the domain of birds and feathered friends. Du Maurier's horror story *The Birds* was published in 1952 and later immortalised by Hitchcock on the Silver Screen in 1963. With her overactive imagination, the thought of kamikaze birds was a little too much more than Mummy could bear. Additionally, Daddy saw clips of *The Birds* as he was growing up and he had no desire to enter the lion's den, so to speak. Fortunately for both parents, I mounted a rescue mission. You see, I was irritable, hot and tired, and provided a perfect excuse for us *not* to fly into the Aviary.

Even though we spent the vast majority of the day in the aquarium, we could easily have spent longer. It was absolutely amazing. Before leaving, we nipped into the restaurant/ cafe. I had some milk, Mummy had a coffee and Daddy had a soft drink. A robot brought our beverages out, but a human waitress had to remove the drinks from the robot to our table, which I think was a flaw in the robo-waiter's techno DNA.

All in all, we very much enjoyed our day in Valencia. Admittedly, we didn't actually see much of Valencia, but, you can't miss what you never saw and I had a great time with Mumma and Dadnad.

If you're interested, here is the information about Valencia, courtesy of the *Horizon* newsletter. If you read this and use a bit of creative licence, you can pretend that you've been to Valencia and its old town.

WELCOME TO VALENCIA

Vibrant Valencia, Spain's third-largest city is a popular and picturesque resort known for its pavement cafes, parties (Las Fallas) and paella. Amongst art and architecture you can see plazas, palaces, churches and cathedrals, before heading to one of the city's white sandy beaches to cool off. Valencia Cathedral displays 3 magnificent portals; one Baroque, one Romanesque and one Gothic. In the new town wander down wide balmy avenues and simply observe and enjoy the Mediterranean way of life. More recent additions to the city include the aesthetically stunning and ultramodern 'City of Arts and Sciences' with its fantastically shaped soaring glass palaces.

On account of the lottery numbers being more important than our favourite feature of the *Britain Today* newspaper, I have added a piece of history. We were most surprised to see that no reference had been made to this event.

TODAY IN HISTORY

On September 8, 2022, Queen Elizabeth II died peacefully at Balmoral Castle in Scotland aged 96 years old. She was Britain's longest serving monarch and was Queen for 70 years and 214 days.

Queen Elizabeth II was pipped to the post of longest reigning monarch in the world by King Louis XIV of France. He put in a healthy effort lasting 72 years and 110 days. Daddy said that Louis became King when he was a boy, so he had a head start on Elizabeth who didn't ascend to the throne until the age of 25. Now, everyone tends to think that a quarter-of-a-century year old person is quite young to become monarch. But, spare a thought for Louis. He became King when he was just 30 months older than I am, so that made him four years and eight months. I certainly wouldn't be ready to grab the sceptre and rule a nation in a bit over three years' time. What were his parents thinking? Well, it turns out his Dad- the imaginatively named King Louis XIII, wasn't doing much thinking as he died aged 41 from tuberculosis. His Mum- Anne of Austria and Queen of France, stuck around until 1666 when she then departed this mortal coil. But she could at least rest, knowing that six years earlier her son had married and secured the throne (because making sure that this regal chair was padlocked down was apparently very important).

Based on the fact that Louis' first years of Kinging were overseen by his mother and godfather, I therefore declare that Queen Elizabeth II is the legitimate holder of the title of longest reigning monarch worldwide, because she started Queening as an adult and not a child under supervision. I'll let you make your own minds up though.

SUPER OLD MASSIVE
MAGNOLIA TREE

09 September

A DAY OF SPANISH HIGHLIGHTS IN CARTAGENA

SUNRISE 07:40
SUNSET 20:17

As with our arrival into Valencia, we watched as Captain Camby steered us into the significant naval port of Cartagena (pronounced Cart-uh-hen-na) in the Murcia region of Spain. It's quite exciting being able to watch the new destination unfurling. Straight away, Mummy and Daddy recognised the maritime association of Cartagena as there was a ship building yard that they were heading straight for, some submarines, some quirky green mountains (or maybe just very large hills) and a beautiful, picture-perfect harbour, all neatly arranged in a natural horseshoe shape. As an added bonus, you could stroll straight off the boat and immediately, bish bash bosh, you were in the heart of Cartagena- no shuttle buses required. Incidentally, there is a Cartagena in Columbia that is affectionately nicknamed The Heroic City, on account of it being the first Columbian City to declare its independence from Spain in 1811. Our Cartagena in España is known rather simply as... Cartagena. But, in fairness, our Cartagena was the first Cartagena to be given this name when it was founded in 227 BC.

To be honest, we thought that Cartagena would be a bit naff. On our original itinerary, we were supposed to be going to Marseille, but the French didn't remember that they were playing host to the Rugby World Cup 2023 and forgot that they had made Marseille Old Town into a designated fan zone. I suspect that today, the ninth of September, there would have been a lot of testosterone zinging about. About ten days before we were due to sail, we got an email to say that Marseille would be closed for business, merci beaucoup. England were playing Argentina at the Stade de Marseille. And if you're interested, England won 27-10. Anyway, not wishing to deprive us of a destination to visit, *P&O Cruises* consulted the map and Cartagena was the alternative replacement destination.

We'd really been looking forward to visiting Marseille- in fact, this was the place that the parents had been most excited to see. From Marseille, the plan was to go to the Chateau d'If, which is the real place that inspired Dumas' *The Count of Monte Cristo*. Mummy had even done some research and we were going to have an excursion to this former prison as our cruise sources had informed us that as we were visiting Marseille on a Sunday, everything would be closed. So, we made our own plans that we then abandoned on learning that our Spanish-French Vacance would now just be a Spanish Sojourn.

Mumma and Dadnad made the mistake of watching an American tourists video of his time in Cartagena. He managed to make this beautiful, elegant city look very drab and industrious. In reality, what we saw was clean, welcoming, and resonating with culture and history as far back as the Roman times, if not further. However, once they'd seen this chaps' video, they were dreading such a waste of a land day. Well, dear Readers, I am pleased to report that they were very wrong about their preconceptions and had to eat a hearty dose of humble pie. You see, Cartagena was a day of highlights for us Musketeers, from our cheap and cheerful boat trip to the scrumptious tapas; seeing the ancient Roman ruins through the pauper's station because the queues were too long and it was incompatible with my buggy; the relaxed, timeless shopping precinct where I didn't feel too overwhelmed, as well as the culture and history, and the sheer surprise of being entirely won over by a place that we expected to be totally dire. My Brontë verdict of Cartagena is that it is a little Spanish secret city find. I liked it a lot and so did Maramis and d'Adtagnan. The sun was shining too (28 degrees C), so we felt positively toasty tropical.

TODAY IN HISTORY

On Sept. 9, 1543, Mary Stuart was crowned Queen of Scots at Stirling Castle, nine months after she was born.

Move over Louis XIV, there's an even more junior monarch than you. History is about to come full circle, folks. Do you remember I mentioned about the Spanish Armada when we were in Cadiz? Well, Mary Queen of Scots was executed for treason at the age of 44 in 1587. Rather awkwardly, once her head and body were no longer one piece, the executioner held up her head to show he'd done his job and then her poor head fell to the ground, leaving him holding just her wig. Wearing wigs was commonplace until 1795 when the British government did what they did best and introduced a brand new tax: the hair powder tax. This is not me pulling your leg, but a real tax that- naturally, people did not want to pay. King George IV decided that he wasn't prepared to pay one guinea annually for the privilege of wearing his wig. In todays money, that's at least £500-00 for your talc.

As you're reading an excellent and informative book, let's take the wage that a worker skilled in the printing trade could expect to earn each year in 1797: the princely sum of £67-00 per annum, leaving him with a £400-00 plus wig tax deficit. No wonder they fell out of fashion. Anyway, this has been a long and winding journey down memory lane that leads me to my point: Mary's execution was the catalyst for the Spanish to launch their Armada a year after her death.

Following an early breakfast, we disembarked and walked up 'Paseo de Alfonso XII'. Lots of street names and places in Spain have an Alfonso in the title. Historically speaking, there's at least twelve Alfonso's. A little retrospective research confirms that there is actually thirteen of them, with Alfonso the Lasts reign ending in 1931. The first Alfonso was almost 1,200 years earlier. Perhaps people weren't as imaginative on the name front? Maybe they needed to borrow Mummy and Daddy's Baby Name book? They know lots of names. Admittedly, they know more boys names as when I was existing in the watery world of Mumma's tum-tum, they knew nothing about me (except that I was their future offspring). Nine out of ten people wrongly predicted that I was a boy. So, Mummy gave up on reading the girls names and just looked at boys names. She and Daddy had a whole list of boy possibilities, but on the off-chance that I wasn't a boy, they had only one pair of names for a girl- my first and middle names.

When Daddy proposed to Mummy, they were on holiday in Spain in a place called Nerja. There, they stood on the Balcon d'Europa, with its commanding views over the Mediterranean Sea and a bronze statue of Alfonso the Something. Daddy took a picture of Mummy next to it. This Alfonso was 5ft 7in, so Mummy was taller than a Spanish king! Funnily enough, it turns out that this was Alfonso XII- the same Alfonso of the Cartagena street name fame. He didn't king for very long- just nine years before his demise from tuberculosis at the age of 27. Still, he was very popular. Perhaps the few years that he spent in exile added to his mystique?

The promenade along Cartagena's harbour front was lovely. Apart from the atrocious blaring music, meant to entice the crowds to watch the bonkers person with the water jet shoes ascend to heights of up to 45 ft (13.7 m). It was so loud you couldn't even hear your own thoughts, let alone what anyone was saying to you. Everywhere we looked, people seemed baffled by the incongruity of this music with the beauty and sense of calm stillness that somehow emanates from the soul of this city. Give me some Spanish guitar and castanets any day.

We had a little stroll into the city entrance, but this was a popular spot for the thousands disembarking the ship. Shortly after, Daddy announced that he needed the toilet. Luckily for him, Mummy is observant and had spotted some portaloo's, so Daddy braved one of those. The only thing was, the toilets were right under an industrial boom-boom-boom speaker, behind the stall for the water jet shoes company. Whilst Daddy was doing his business, Mummy and I wondered across the square to look at a huge statue of a man crying in exasperation at the awfulness of the music. Oh, now I feel bad. It turns out that the sad statue is showing his sorrow for victims of terrorism. The bad music was a coincidence that set my imagination up a little too well.

When Daddy exited the toilet, he found us by the statue and reported back that he had been to 'toilet hell' (direct quote), as the portaloo was vibrating from the bass and music. Apparently, it was also as hot as hell on a cold day, but pleasingly aroma free. Daddy said that the music was so loud it was like being at the front of the stage of a Who concert. I'm not quite sure who The Who? are, but I'm guessing that they're a band who like questions and grammar.

On a different subject, Cartagena have developed an initiative called the CAC. I know this because Mummy tore the information off of the complimentary map when that was surplus to requirements and stuck the little relevant bit into my journal. Cartagena calls their pledge the 'Cruises Friend Shop'. Not wishing to ostracise our other European friends, they helpfully have the title in German: Kreuzfahrt Handel Freund; French: Commerce Ami des Croisières, and; Spanish, of course: Comercio Amigo de los Cruceros (CAC).

Considering we are now starting to read with more frequency that there are places that don't want cruise ships to dock in their ports- notably Venice in Italy, and Flam in Norway, this little Cruises Friend Shop was precisely that- a friendly welcome. I can understand why Venice and Flam don't necessarily want the colossal mega-ships to pull up as the influx of day visitors- in addition to those that live and work there, or who are holidaying in the area, is immense. At the moment, Cartagena has no such qualms and- unlike Marseille, they pledge to have their shops and establishments open whenever a cruise ship of just 300 or more passengers drops by to say *hola!*. And yes, there is some truth to the myth that cruise passengers don't spend their money when on land. But if you saw the lengthy queues to see the Roman ruins across the day, you would think that there was no truth to the myth of the no-spend cruise visitor. Each time somebody vacated the queue and was admitted to the ruins, a new person was there to join the people rotation.

As you might have guessed, Cartagena is known for its Roman ruins. It wasn't until 1987 that the city discovered they were concealing a Roman amphitheatre, following the demolition of a nineteenth century palace. The Roman theatre is believed to have been able to accommodate about 7,000 viewers and was built at the end of the first century BC, so that's a good while ago. This ruin and museum is now the most visited museum in the Murcia region.

Cartagena's ancient ruins, nestled in the midst of the city.

In terms of Roman ruins, it's still got the novelty factor as it only came to light less than forty years ago.

Interestingly, the website *Murcia Today* recommend a ninety minute visit and say- direct quote: 'sensible children with a certain degree of maturity will enjoy the experience'. On this basis alone, we ruled out a visit as I don't think that I have the prerequisite degree of maturity. Yes, I'm a senior babe and part-time toddler. No, I'm probably not sensible enough to be classified as a sensible child as I'm still at the stage where I will put everything into my mouth, which is probably the opposite of sensible. As you know, the queues were sizeable, so we set off on foot to explore the city. Accidentally, we stumbled across the exit of the ruins, which is right by the amphitheatre. So we drank in the history from the cheap seats and in the process saved ourselves €30-00.

I've included a decent sketch of the ancient ruins. Unfortunately for us, our shots of the ruins are obscured by the bars of an industrial fence. Even better for you, the image of the ruins are people free, which is an added bonus for us too. Ours were peppered with people in every available space, making it almost impossible to have a clear view of this slice of Roman history.

WELCOME TO CARTAGENA

An ancient city with a name to match - it was founded more than 2,200 years ago by Carthaginian leader Hasbrudal - Cartagena is now one of Spain's busiest commercial centres. Step ashore here,

though, and you are immediately aware
of its rich history. In fact, you see it even
as you cruise towards the harbour as
this is flanked by towering fortresses.
Then, in the centre of the old town,
you will find the original Carthaginian
castle and sections of the old city walls.
But Cartagena is also a city which moves
with the times hence the new harbourfront
development which includes the unique
National Museum of
Underwater Archaeology.

We poked our heads into a couple of churches. They were pleasant- the Spanish certainly do like their iconography! We also saw an amazing magnolia tree that must have been at least a hundred years old. It was practically the size of a house. No exaggeration.

One of our favourite activities was the forty minute boat ride around the massive horseshoe harbour and some of the coastline. It was brilliant and we would highly recommend. So that everyone knew that we were tourists, the boat was imaginatively named 'Barco Turístico', which helpfully translates as Tourist Boat. For the total sum of €12-00, we got to enjoy this leisurely trip across choppy waters. There was even a real-life pirate to welcome us aboard that looked suspiciously like Jack Sparrow. Lots of Spanish children dressed as pirates and princesses also boarded the little tourist boat, but they weren't on there for long and all got off at a stop about ten minutes later with

Captain Jack. Then, bar for about a dozen or so other people, we basically had the boat to ourselves. I really enjoyed it and so did the parents. To celebrate, I demonstrated my ever-improving walking skills.

Honestly, our boat trip was worth every cent. It even had a commentary that was in English. Did you know: on a clear day, from Cartagena, you can see Algeria? And did you know: Algeria is on a different continent called Africa? Actually, no, hold on. Mummy must have misheard. I think he must have said Almeria, which would make more sense geographically. I've just checked out our postcard map of Spain and I'm fairly certain that Mummy was wrong. I don't think anyones eyesight would be good enough to see Africa after all. I don't even think binoculars would be man enough for the job of continent spotting. Still, we enjoyed some magnificent views and top-notch family time. Plus, we got to see Arvia from lots of different vantage points without lots of people or buildings in the way, which was a novelty. I also got to go on a ship and a boat- two sea-going vessels in one day. And, the bestest bit of all was that- unlike the ship, our little boat was almost devoid of people once the pirates and princesses had walked the plank. Thanks- as ever, must once again go to *P&O Cruises* for the complimentary muffin.

We had a fantastic tapas lunch- opting to visit two adjacent bars. It was a triumph and our food highlight so far this holiday. Mummy and Daddy enjoyed beer and octopus salad- far superior to the Galician offering, as well as fresh anchovies and salmon. It was all very lovely and relaxed. I also got to enjoy some tasty, authentic Spanish breadsticks that we'd bought on our visit to the local supermercado. I think that they might be my favourite breadsticks yet, and I've tried a lot. I really am a breadstick connoisseur, from Greek to Italian and English styles, the Spanish ones were on another breadstick level. We were given a tip about the tapas places by an older English couple from our cruise who hopped aboard the tourist boat after we told them about it. It was a most fortuitous chance encounter as the tapas was bueno, bueno, bueno!

It turns out you can buy most things in a Spanish supermarket, but not glue. Industrial silicone? Yep. Freshly baked breadsticks? Yep. A hip flask? Yes, of course. Tile adhesive? Most certainly. Glue? Absolutely not, are you mad?

Because we had time, we wandered up and down the marble pavements and streets, venturing intermittently off the main roads and onto quieter parallel streets. It looked very traditional Parisian. Everywhere you looked, there was beauty. Even buildings with nothing more than a crumbling or demolished back behind the first metre of disintegrating frontage were maintaining the historic façade whilst modernising behind the scenes. Perhaps Cartagena has some UNESCO status? Or maybe they just care about things looking as nice as they can.

We popped into a few shops and I bought a rubber duck to add to my collection of four animal bath time friends (a crab, a whale, a fish and a turtle). I thought my little duck would be a super souvenir for me, but was slightly disappointed to find that if you turned it upside down, there in teeny tiny print are the innocuous words 'Made in China'. Shame. Still, if you're interested, the rubber duck is bright yellow and has wings, a wand, and some white hair tied into a low bun. I have named her Fairy Duckmother. Daddy bought a couple of hats and Mummy got a jasper bracelet.

One of the shops we nipped into was a Euroland style place that had glass floors over Roman ruins. The history and culture beneath our feet was in sharp contrast to all the bric-à-brac on the shelves. It was a total juxtaposition. Culture aside though, whilst Mummy was searching for some glue and a spare notebook, Daddy and I got distracted by a vast collection of balls. The one that we were drawn to was a large rainbow ball. Because it made us so happy, Daddy bought it for me as a present. What a result! I was genuinely chuffed. Riding high on my rainbow ball purchase, I didn't think that the day could get any better. But then we went into a few other shops and made a detour via a frozen yoghurt store. Oh my goodness, what delights am I tasting? It was torturously scrumptious, on account of it being so tasty delicious and yet icy cold.

Once back aboard Arvia, I had a play in the nursery and then an unsuccessful dinner. It consisted of salmon, potatoes and peas. At home, this is a firm favourite, but at sea, it was unfortunately too over-salted and over-seasoned for my delicate, juvenile tastebuds. Still, the strawberry jelly that followed was a reasonable level of compensation for the savoury failure.

I should have mentioned something else earlier about Marseille. From multiple different sources on-board the ship, we have been informed that things in Marseille are not all that très bien at the moment. Apparently, there's a lot of civil unrest and protesting going on. I'm not entirely sure what the blazes the issues are, but I'm guessing that it's one of the big three, as denoted by the tricolour flag of France: fraternité, egalité et liberté (they translate as brotherhood, equality and freedom). With my logical Brontë brain, I'd translate these three things as fraternisation *fraternité* (with friend and foe), eagles *egalité* (because that is what that word reminds me of) and libra's *liberté* (as in the scales and the zodiac). You see, the libra's are weighing up the issues on their see-saw scales whilst sending eagle scouts out to fraternise with those on the streets of Marseille in order to establish precisely what the matter is. So, there we have it folks, etymology is the key to translation. At the very least, it makes things a darn sight more exciting.

As a one year old wearer of clothes, I take my job of trying to get through as many as I can in one 24 hour window very seriously. So seriously, in fact, that Mummy had to go to a hitherto undiscovered place on the ship called the laundrette. That's basically a fancy word for clothing machine cleaners. I supervised- of course, as Mum loaded up the washing machine. Unfortunately, I couldn't really help as much as I do at home as these machines were very different to what I'm used to. I'm not really sure that Mummy knew what she was pressing either, because in the end and in exasperation, she pushed a load of buttons in quick succession until the machine sprang to life. The funny thing was, even though Mummy went to the launderette at about eight o'clock at night, it was busy and most of the machines were in use. I found myself pondering a deep and meaningful question: apart from Mummy's travelling with a one year old, who are all these people that do washing on their holidays? I mean, hello! You're on holiday!

In the bath before bed, I introduced Fairy Duckmother to the mismatched gang of ocean dwellers. And then, I polished off some first rate milk before bidding adios to the day. I left Mummy and Daddy to watch a film and hang the washing, post-tumble, that was slightly damp and verging on tepid, as opposed to hot and fluffy. You can't beat parenthood for all the thrills that a one year old can initiate and share. And on that note, I bid you farewell until tomorrow comes.

10 September

THESE BOOTS ARE MADE FOR WALKING

SUNRISE 07:29
SUNSET 20:12

Today is a sea day. Or as I prefer to look at it; a rest day. When you've got a limited time ashore, the tendency is to try to cram as much as you can into your allocated visit window. So, having had two consecutive land days, we were all in need of a relax. This meant that instead of a 06:45 alarm that is then snoozed for a quarter of an hour as Mummy wrestles her consciousness and fights the urge to return to slumber, the alarm did not start its merry tune until 07:30. I know, it's positively indulgent.

Before said alarm could go off this morning, yours truly stirred from behind my tropical travel screen (more commonly known as The Great Divide. Thanks to the magnetic ceiling and the loan of some magnetic hooks from our hairdresser, the shower curtain enabled us to create two bedroom pods. You'd never have thought that you could subdivide a tiddly cabin, but where there's a will there's a way! The only compromise that had to be made was that when my curtain wall was up, there was no longer any access to the balcony as I was blocking the door with my bed. It wasn't intentional, but that was the only place for me to go).

So, this morning, no early alarms had been set, but the parents forgot that I am a creature of habit. Or at least they forgot, until I announced my presence with a rustle of the sheets and gargantuan yawn (where I practically inhaled all the remaining oxygen in the cabin), at 07:27. I was thinking of Mummy and Daddy, honestly, I was. I didn't want complacency to set in and was concerned by the lack of movement from beyond The Great Divide.

It turns out that I needn't have worried, for Mummy was already awake and indulging in her favourite pastime of resting her eyes. Resting them where, I don't know. On the nightstand? In her handbag? Sometimes, I find it best not to ask too many questions and simply accept that the ways of grown-ups are one of life's greatest mysteries to those of us in single figures. My wake-up call didn't quite rise Daddy from Slumbertown, but he awoke when Mumma declared that 'sleep time's over', and gestured in my direction. You're welcome, anytime I can be of service, just ask.

Gee whizz. There are clothes everywhere in every available hanging space. It smells like a launderette in the room. The bathroom is the main source of clothing captivity and may as well be a clothes warehouse. The shower is now out of action as it has been commandeered and reincarnated as an airer. Fortunately, I didn't have to use the toilet, because if I did, I'd be struggling. I thought it best to follow my earlier role of asking no questions. I'm all for a simple life.

After breakfast, Mummy disappeared like a professional magician. Instead of bringing me with her, she chose to take all the clean clothes, which was odd behaviour. Why choose clothes instead of me, a brilliant babe? There's really no contest in my book. Luckily for me, Mumma left me with my best friend- Dadnad, in the cabin.

I feel, dear Diary, that I should confide that I'm worried about Mummy. You see, even though we're on holiday, she returned to the clothes cleaning machines room to go and do the ironing. Yes, you did read that correctly: my Mummy was ironing on holiday. Whatever next? I can only imagine that she must have ironing withdrawal symptoms because- let me reiterate this once again: she felt the urge to iron whilst on holiday. Is this normal behaviour? I really don't know. I've not been on Earth long enough to know, but my instinct tells me that this is out of character for someone who is supposed to be relaxing. Although- in fairness, in my role as a professional one year old, I do put a daily limit on the levels of relaxation as fun is far more of an important pursuit. Always.

But in all seriousness, I'm wondering if I should book Mummy a place with the IA. That, my friend, is Ironers Anonymous, to those in the know. The mission of the IA Institute is to free the ironer from the incessant urge to press and steam ones clothing. Those at the IA believe that there is not enough time in the world to dedicate to unnecessary ironing and aim to liberate the unfortunate ironoholic.

One moment, please.

Daddy's just informed me that Mummy does not meet the criteria to qualify for the IA. He said that it wasn't a compulsion to steam and press, but that Mummy was ironing out of necessity. It was the only way to get yesterdays partially dried garments totally wardrobe putawayable. My mistake. I must really learn to stop jumping to conclusions.

At 11:00, we went to *Shaun the Sheep* story time in the Club House. The thing was, the girl telling the story lost my attention within about forty seconds. Not long after, the other bambinos stopped paying attention. She was supposed to have a *Shaun the Sheep* story projected onto a big screen, but appeared to be having a serious technical malfunction and was unable to flip the image from her laptop to the screen. So, she instead read from a book with pictures that you could not see, unless you were sat in her lap. Still, before I had a chance to dwell on the fact that I couldn't see what she was pointing at, a real life human-sized Shaun walked into the room, which was rather exciting. Of course, I played it cool. Perhaps a little too cool. I was certainly a lot more nonchalant than the parents.

We had a few pictures taken, because why would we not? I mean, it was a giant sheep. These opportunities don't come around every day.

Once we'd got our photos, we left Shaun to do whatever oversize sheep do as he was interrupting a very important moment of the day: nap time. And both my nap buddy and I were sorely in need. Mummy took advantage of our snooze time and used it to catch up on her writing.

Later, we completed four circuits of the promenade deck and then got changed for an early tea. I had chicken, potato, vegetable blitz. It was actually quite tasty. Hallelujah! And then, Mummy went to see a Take That show at the theatre called 'Greatest Days'. This meant that I had some extra bonus Daddy-Daughter time, so we did what we do best and walked. And walked. And walked. I practically walked myself into bed.

Mummy enjoyed her sixty-minute solo theatre trip. She ended up sitting next to a lady who was a big Take That fan and was singing along to Every. Single. Song. She said that this was her fourth time watching the show, but her first time watching it when floating at sea. She was a solo passenger out of choice, whereas Mummy was a solo passenger out of necessity.

HEADLINERS THEATRE COMPANY PRESENTS - GREATEST DAYS

Greatest Days by Tim Firth, The Official Take That Musical, is an adaptation of the acclaimed West End musical The Band. The show features the songs of Take That

and a beautiful story by Olivier
Award-winning writer Tim Firth,
all brought to life on stage by an amazing
cast. Please note - performance run time is
60 minutes. (This show will be repeated
on the 11 September).

When Mummy got back to the cabin, she told us that it was so good that she even shed a tear. And then, she promptly booked Daddy a virtual ticket so he could watch it tomorrow and see if he would shed a tear. I highly doubt he will, as when Mummy asked Daddy if he liked Take That, he said 'kind of'. The lady sat next to Mummy cried enough for the both of them, though. Like I said, she was a big fan.

Due to me being a youngster, we missed out on what I'm sure would have been a thrilling presentation called the 'Pre Owned Rolex Talk'. If we had been able to attend, I would much rather discuss the unowned Rolex watches than a hand-me-down. Owned or pre owned though, I still wouldn't have bought one. Daddy's got a replica knock-off Rolex from Singapore that I've been promised once I'm eighteen. If anything, that's got more history than an anonymous pre owned ship Rolex. Mine's been pre owned by my Daddy and therefore, its value is incalculable. It's also cobbled together with whatever the pirate watchmakers could find. So there may actually be 1% Rolex in there, which is an added plus. It certainly isn't worthless. Unless you're a criminal, in which case it is quite literally of inestimable worth and on par with a legitimate Rolex, which are sought after because the demand does not match the supply and exceeds it significantly. Mummy was so impressed with the craftsmanship of Daddy's Rolexeo (what I am calling a Rolex copy), that she recently suggested he auction it. Luckily for Dad, it's got my sticker on.

TODAY IN HISTORY

On Sept 10, 1669, Henrietta Maria,
French wife of Charles I of England, died
near Paris. Henrietta Street, London
WC2, is named after her. In 1855, the
Russian Black Sea base of Sebastopol fell
to Anglo-French forces after an 11-month
siege. In 1897, taxi driver George Smith
was fined £1, making him the first person
in Britain to be convicted for
drink-driving.

Today, in the decade that is the 2020s, the amount of people convicted of drink driving related offences stands at roughly 85,000 annually. This is just in England and Wales, and excludes Scotland and Northern Ireland. Perhaps surprisingly, approximately 85% of the 85,000 convictions are male. Fines have increased a fair bit since Smith was charged £1·00 in 1897 (about £160·00 with inflation in todays money).

If someone was reckless enough to drink and drive now, they risk a three month stint at His Majesty's Pleasure in prison, as well as a fine of up to £2,500·00 and a driving ban. To help the government work out how wealthy they might become, based on 85,000 convictions at £1,500-00 each (I'm being lenient), that nets the coffers a staggering £127,500,000-00. And the government say that crime doesn't pay. Call me cynical, but I think that the Chancellor of the Exchequer may beg to differ. Then again, the minor figure of £127 million worth of fines may just be a tiny sprinkle on the UK alcohol duty that netted approximately £12.4 billion in 2022-2023. That, is a lot of alcohol. So much in fact, that it equates to about 2.5% of the total GDP of the national income. Maybe a life on the strait and narrow is okay? I for one would never drink and drive when milk drunk. I'd just go and sleep it off.

The captain today told a funny anecdote. 'Did you know that the Canary Islands don't have any canaries?' No, I did not. 'And did you know that the Virgin islands… don't have any canaries either?' Eh? You've lost me. I'm not sure why yellow songbirds are so amusing, but all the adults laughed knowingly, so it must be some sort of in-joke for those over sixteen. As I said earlier, it's best not to seek explanations and simply let the adults adult, as adulting makes them very happy, I have observed.

IT'S A MOUNTAIN
NOT A HILL

11 September

BEWARE THE
PICKPOCKET

SUNRISE 07:29
SUNSET 20:12

Hello Barcelona. First impressions as we tethered up in port? Very interesting. And it's massive. There's lots to see and lots of variety from views of the harbour to lush, green rocky hills, to houses that reminded the parents of Athens, and sailing boats alongside shipping containers that- in proportion to the giant cranes scattered across the sides of the commercial port, reminded me of my *Duplo* blocks (I'm too young for a *Lego* analogy as *Lego* is still small enough to make the leap from hand to mouth). I would say that what we saw was definitely a visual smorgasbord of delights. Interestingly, Daddy is allergic to the word smorgasbord. When used outside of a food context, he involuntarily recoils. One could say I've chosen it on purpose. But I will neither confirm nor deny such speculation.

As Arvia was docking and all the paperwork was being filled out by the important people, we watched as three ant-sized tug boats surrounded a tower block of a shipping container. The one at the front guided it forward, bound to this ridiculously large floating skyscraper, by a relatively thin piece of rope compared to the size of what it was pulling. This tug driver was the VIP of the operation, being at the front. Quite possibly, even the brains of the tugboat gang. And then, there was another tug in the middle of the container ship. He wasn't attached to the vessel they were moving. His job was to keep the container in line. Periodically, if he thought that the ship was stepping out of line, he'd go wide to the right and then full throttle back to the left and into the boat. I'm not sure if the skyscraper noticed when the flying ant landed on it, but adjustments always seemed to be made. This middle guy was the one who was a stickler for order. He was the army corporal of the operation.

Parallel to the middle tug was the harbour wall, so I don't think there was a tug on that side. This leads us to the third member of the tug trio: the one bringing up the rear. This guy is the muscle of the operation. He's like a cross between the most powerful ocean-bound mammal and the strongest land mammal, making this muscle head a whalephant. You could practically see the steam coming off of him with the huge frothy water in his wake from the exertion of pushing such a heffalump of a seagoing creation. Mummy was absorbed in the theatre of the tugboat trio for a very long time. Until I reminded her that my tummy was empty and in need of some milk. And just like that, she vacated the balcony and the spell was broken.

We have an overnight stay in Barcelona, so today we've done our own thing and been sweaty, hiking tourists. Tomorrow, we plan to be more dignified and-hopefully, keep the perspiration at bay, as we're going to experience the delights of the city from the comfort of our air-conditioned coach.

Today, it was a virtual certainty that we would fall victim to some sticky-fingered pickpockets. So many guests informed us of this criminal magnitude that we felt like we were entering a contagious den of inequity. People advised us to keep all jewellery on the ship in the safe. So off came the wedding rings and Mummy's watch because Daddy said it was too twinkly and might attract the thieves, like magpies. From a distance, they wouldn't know that Mummy's watch is probably worth about £5-00, especially since I've been on the scene and dropping it with my ever-expanding arsenal of motor skills, adding to the scratches that Mummy has made independently. No, the would-be pickpockets would be dazzled by the sun bouncing off of Mummy's watch and- in turn, reach the natural conclusion that we were prime targets and secretly harbouring a lot of priceless jewels and trinkets.

I've been led to believe that I'm priceless, which is concerning because I rather like my Mummy and Daddy and wouldn't want to be sold on the open market for priceless goods. Or worse; the dark web. I'm not up for sale. Fortunately, I have an exemplary burglar alarm inbuilt. When a piercing scream is required, I'm the kiddie. And if that wasn't enough, the pushchair is so darn fiddly and practically requires a degree to operate, that nobody is getting away with me quickly.

Before we'd even left the boat, people were telling us that Barcelona is renowned for its pickpockets. Apparently, they're some of the finest in the world. Although, I'm not sure if that is an accolade that the city would like. Still, it appears that Barcelona has a reputation as the captain warned people to be vigilant. Plus, a feature in the *Horizon* advised guests not to wear excessive jewellery.

BARCELONA PICKPOCKETS - THINK SAFE WHEN ASHORE

Guests are advised to keep to the main tourism areas and be vigilant whilst ashore. Young pickpockets operate in groups in the busy streets. We recommend that you do not wear excessive amounts of jewellery or expensive watches and keep all hand or beach bags close to your body. We do not encourage you to take large amounts of cash or currency ashore with you if not required.

Sobering stuff.

Yes, I say this gravely. If we didn't have our pockets picked, our neighbours in the cabin next door would. I'll be honest, it was a bleak welcome. Couple that with the fact that today is the National Day of Catalonia, so, a public holiday, meaning that the city would be ultra busy. In addition, there are four independence rallies and a taxi strike, all scheduled to take place today, on the first of our two-day visit. All of this would be taking place in the main tourist areas and therefore a mecca for would-be pocket plunderers.

Once the shuttle bus dropped us off, we were on our own. Consequently, we opted to go to the destinations that would be quieter and safer, because otherwise we'd be sitting ducks. Even if we tried to blend in, we still looked like bewildered tourists with the rabbit-in-the-headlights look (as standard), and a patchwork tan. Having been to the beach, I can verify that our tans would have indeed confirmed our visitor status as those on the beaches had all-over tans. And when I say 'all-over', I mean in every little nook and cranny. We even saw two winkles and plenty of nips on display on both the male and female of the species. My young eyes were so surprised by the public nudity that I promptly fell asleep. I didn't want to risk any further indecent exposure reaching my retinas.

CATALONIA DAY

The National Day of Catalonia is a day-long festival and one of its official national symbols, celebrated annually on 11 September.

It commemorates the fall of Barcelona during the War of the Spanish Succession in 1714 and the subsequent loss of Catalan institutions and laws. In recent years this day has been marked by political demonstrations organised by supporters of independence from Spain. During our stay in Barcelona you may find that some shops, bars and restaurants may be closed and public transport could have delays due to the celebrations.

Alongside this, Catalan independence groups plan to demonstrate in central Barcelona, 11 September 2023, to mark Catalan National Day. Pro-independence groups, led by the Catalan National Assembly, will gather in four separate locations in the city and then march to a common rally point, Plaza España. We have been advised that this should not effect your visit but we do suggest you avoid large crowds.

During our time in Barcelona, taxi drivers associated with La Élite Taxi Barcelona intend to hold a taxi-caravan in order to protest against a fine that was imposed by the regional government of Catalunya to the union.

If you're wondering how much La Élite Taxi Barcelona was fined, it was €123,000-00. They didn't like the new kids on the block- Uber, and were pressuring their drivers not to use the 'ride-hailing' platforms. It goes a bit deeper than that, but that's the gist of it. Interestingly, taxis in Barcelona are cheaper than a lot of other European cities. Per kilometre on the meter, in Barcelona, you could expect to pay about 15% less than you would in London or Paris. Even more interestingly, Barcelona taxis are cheaper than Uber by about 15%. We don't use taxis very much at home. Actually, what am I talking about? We *never* use taxis at home as you practically require a second mortgage to cover the fare. We also don't use Uber for one simple reason: it has not crossed the Solent and made it to the Isle of Wight. No, I tell a lie. Even if Uber did paddle across the Solent, we're still not going to use it. We always seem to get taken advantage of in taxis, so wherever possible, we avoid using them. We didn't break our own rule today, instead choosing leg power over motor power.

Instead of going to the main city centre- Las Ramblas, or the Gothic quarter, we headed to Montjuïc to use not one, but two different cable cars. (We also intended to take the funicular, but gave up searching for it). We were not robber-friendly, having opted to leave virtually everything on the ship- including Mummy's handbag. This was a small, compact offering, with a diagonal cross body strap. But it was sadly vetoed as the criminals would apparently just cut it off. Begrudgingly, she left it behind in the cabin because when Daddy asked Mummy what she kept in her handbag, the first thing she said was 'lip balm'. This was followed by purse, phone and pen. Mummy has more pens in bags than anyone else I know and lots of notebooks, on account of her being the worlds greatest (as yet) undiscovered writer. She needs these things for The Big Idea, which could strike at any given time. Anyway, because 'lip balm' was the first item specified, Mummy conceded that the bag wasn't entirely essential. We needn't have worried though as we returned to the ship with all that we departed with. I can't help but think that we concerned ourselves with this more than we needed to as those naked beach people didn't seem to give it a second thought as they had no pockets. Well, at least none that I know of.

WELCOME TO BARCELONA

The Catalonian capital of Barcelona provides a vivid mix of ancient and modern but is probably best known for the bizarre Art Nouveau architecture of Antonio Gaudí, in particular the iconic Sagrada Família, Europe's most extraordinary - and still unfinished - cathedral. Boosted by hosting the Olympic Games in 1992, Barcelona's Old Port area has been transformed into a thriving area of cafés and restaurants. From there, it is an easy stroll up the famous Ramblas to the old town. Las Ramblas is thronged with street entertainers, stalls and bars and is most lively at night and weekends.

Barcelona: famous for an unfinished building. A bit of an odd thing to be known for, in my book. Mummy is famous for half-finished cups of tea, but she doesn't have the same level of fame as this city. I suppose, the main difference between Mummy and the cathedral is that Mummy can always make a fresh cup of tea. The Barcelonian's can't scale down their ambitions and they cannot ask their chief architect as he is- rather inconveniently, dead. The one thing that Mummy and the cathedral do have in common is their inability to finish the job in hand. When I asked Daddy if they'd ever finish the Sagrada Família, he said 'no'- without hesitation. Here's an expanded no with Dadnad's explanation: 'its incompletion *is* the advert'. If it's a finished building, then it immediately loses its USP (that's Unique Selling Point). And it might also mean that they're hit with a hefty tax bill, once the building is deemed finito.

After a bracing hike up the Montjuïc and to Miramar station, we took the cable car over the harbour and down to the Torre San Sebastià on Barceloneta. The parents paid €20-00 each for a return ticket (on account of me being a babe, I was complimentary). Listen to me, I sound like I know what I'm talking about. I'll just take a small moment to bask in my professional tourist status before continuing.

Okay, I'm ready.

Montjuïc is classified as a hill in Spain. Now, I know that sounds a bit disappointing, but I would like to assure you that it is more than just a hill. It's a flipping massive hill. Or, if you need more persuading, it's a prominent hill and offers the highest viewpoint in the city, standing at 565 feet (173 m) above sea level. The

Sagrada Família has the silver medal for the city's second highest construction as Gaudí used to say that 'no man-made construction should be taller than God's creation'. This natural creation is often described as shallow and broad, but in our experience, we must have found the deep and steep parts because the incline to the cable car was practically vertical. And I'm really not exaggerating that much.

Montjuïc is home to two cable cars. The first one we took- the Teleférico del Puerto Barcelona, was built in 1931 (at times, it felt like it was of that vintage. The jolt at the towers was a moment that made my tum-tum fall into the soles of my feet). The red cable cars hold about twelve people, squished in and on a first name basis by the end of the ride that takes you up to roughly 230 feet (70 m) above the city and port. The Port Cable Car (Aeri del Puerto- literally 'Port Air') had a middle stop called Torre de Jaume I, but that was closed. This tower is situated right next to the coach drop-off, which would have been rather convenient. So, we looked down with bemusement and then carried on our merry aerial way until we reached the end of the line at Torre Sant Sebastià.

Due to not being able to find a gentle slope to amble up prior to boarding the cable car at the Mirimar Station, Mummy and Daddy had to have an impromptu workout and carry me, the omnipresent nappy bag with all my paraphernalia, and my pushchair, about a hundred stairs up. These ones were shallow and broad and painfully never ending when Mummy and Daddy were laden down with me and the luggage. If the parents had known where they were going, round the corner they would have found a nice gentle wheel friendly walkway. But it was too hot to go searching for the easy option, so they took the sweat-busting shortcut. My job was simple: to supervise the operation. And then, once we'd reached the communal cable car station and descended some narrow steps to reach the actual car, I sat on Mummy's lap and watched as the city quickly gave way to the ocean. Halfway through the journey, I switched parents and stared out of the window with Dadnad- from a safe distance. One wrong move and we would have found out if I could fly or not. I didn't dare look down. And then, we reached the end tower and took a teeny tiny lift that whizzed us slowly back to Earth.

With our feet back on terra firma, we explored the not-as-historic-as-we-thought promenade of La Platja de Sant Sebastià. It had a contemporary look, with its wide sweeping promenade that seamlessly transitioned from a walkway and into the golden sands of the beach on the sea side, whilst being flanked by fantastic open-air outdoor pools and eateries, concealing the beach from the roadside.

Until Barcelona played host to the 1992 Olympic Games, Barcelona was a city with virtually no coastline. Instead, what lined the coast was industry overfill. So, the city made the very wise decision to convert this land into a dazzling coastline, creating a seaside area offering 2.79 miles (4.5 km) of beach, including sand that has been imported from Egypt. Now that I know this, it makes a lot more sense as to why we had to cross the port and so much commercial space: because the beach was redundant commercial space. Hosting the Olympics, I would suggest, has proved to be most fortuitous for Barcelona's fortunes and aesthetic coastal appeal.

Today, the sea was as flat as the tum-tum-Tummerson's we saw on display. There were more ripples on the people working out in the open-air Miami-style beach gym, than there was on the sea. The beach provided multiple opportunities for people-watching, of which I am very good at. Being a junior member of the human race, makes me an excellent participant in a staring contest as I can keep my eyes open for a super long time, without feeling the need to blink.

We strolled along this beach, to the overly large building that you see. Here, we witnessed all levels of clothing optional people in pursuit of the perfect non-patchwork tan. Somehow, this image doesn't actually do the beauty of this beach justice. It really was a sublime specimen of beach. But I suppose I wanted to show you how incongruous such a giant construction looks, directly adjacent to the beach.

A lady with a purposeful walk at the beach of Barceloneta, beneath the towering hotel shaped like a sail.

Beneath our postcard picture (not featured here, but it's in my actual physical journal for prosperity. In case you're curious as to what it looks like, it's very similar to the photo sketch I've chosen) it says *Platja de la Barceloneta. Edifici Vela.* The word platja means 'beach' and La Barceloneta is a neighbourhood in Barcelona, literally translating as Little Barcelona. Edifici Vela is the huge skyscraper building at the end of the platja. Edifici means building and Vela is the nickname that the building has; it means 'sail', as in sailboat. Even though it's a hotel called the W Barcelona Hotel (yes, an underwhelming name choice), it is locally known as the Sail Hotel, due to its resemblance to a sail filled with a hearty gust of wind.

A mere 65 feet (20 m) from the water's edge, Hotel Vela was completed in September 2009 at a cost of an estimated €200 million and features 473 rooms. It's going to take a lot of bums in beds to recoup the build cost, break even, and start turning a profit. But then, what can I know about economics when I'm not even two yet?

After we'd had a nice refreshing drink and walk in both directions of the promenade, we stopped in a local supermarket to pick up some tonic and then headed back to the cable car. We had a much longer wait, but eventually we ascended the lift to the top of the cable car, whereupon we found... another queue. This one was hidden from view. Mummy changed my undies in the designated baby/ disabled cubicle. There wasn't actually that much space to move in there, mostly due to the fact that this areas primary purpose was to house all manner of cleaning chemicals and contraptions. Its secondary purpose was as a toilet and baby changing facility. Anyway, after waiting for what felt like a good half an hour in very, very toasty conditions, we took the cable car back to the Mirimar station.

Once I'd been hoisted up the stairs, Mummy and Daddy had a photo of the three of us taken from the viewpoint and then, having ticked off cable car number one, we celebrated with a single communal scoop of natural ice cream in a tub with a miniature shovel. As you would expect, it was totally delicious. We ate this in the Gardens of Mirimar and then had a stroll through the pretty landscaped areas. We also admired the 5* Mirimar Hotel- a beautiful, historic building with a commanding presence thanks to the choice to retain the former palace façade to the frontage during its renovation. The building was built in 1929 for the Universal Expo- the second time the city had hosted this event (the first was in 1888). As with the Hotel Vela, Hotel Mirimar is also billed as a luxury establishment, so therefore the sort of place that we three will look at and admire from the outside, without dropping in. The fancier the establishment, the less toddler compatible it becomes. Still, it was a sight to behold and offered a wonderful contrast to the mirrored modernity of the beach hotel.

Following our rest and absorption of the atmosphere and views, the parents and I then set off with a renewed spring in our step in pursuit of cable car number two: Telefèric de Montjuïc (also known as the Montjuïc cable car). This second cable car had smaller pod-like cabins for about six to eight people and was actually built on the mountain to take you to the castle at the top. It's just a shame we failed to realise that there was a castle at the finish line.

The castles' first incarnation was as a military enclave when it started castling in 1640 for the ominous and grim sounding Reaper's War. Some people call it The Catalan Revolt. As you know, the principality of Catalan includes citizens on the French and Spanish sides. My understanding is that the French wanted the Spanish side of Catalonia and the Spanish said 'absolutamente no'. Yes, I am simplifying things, but I'm only one. So, argy-bargy went on from 1640 until

1659 when the Treaty of the Pyrenees in 1659 was agreed. This basically decreed that the land north of the Pyrenees was part of France and the land to the south was Spanish. Fast-forward several centuries, and the castle now belongs to the citizens of Barcelona, as of 2007.

Gee whizz, if that first hill with all the intermittent steps to get to cable car number one wasn't steep enough- or long enough, the ascent to cable car number two certainly made up for it! Mummy and Daddy were melting as quickly as my ice cream had. Even I was perspiring gently, and I was just being pushed in the perambulator. I felt for them, I really did. Unfortunately though, my vocabulary isn't developed enough to offer words of encouragement, so I just smiled empirically and contentedly as required, which seemed to do the trick.

It turns out that there are three cable car stations to the Telefèric de Montjuïc. Unlike cable car number one, all three were open. Unbeknownst to us, if we'd have changed our direction of travel soon after beginning our post ice-cream hike, we would have reached the Parc de Montjuïc in a jiffy. Instead, we powered on up to the midpoint of the cable car and boarded it at the Placa del Mirador. We paid €15-00 for Mumma and the same for Dadnad. Once again, I was a delightful complimentary bonus and cost precisely zero cents. After a short wait, we hopped into our own private cable car cabin and stayed on without leaping off. It was amazing and one of my favourite things. It offered a beautiful birds eye view of the city, but it didn't feel like you were in a city thanks to all the greenery and plants up the mountain (yes, mountain, not hill). The world somehow seems so much more beautiful when you've got space around you and aren't squashed in like a tin of sardines. The ride was a lot smoother than the first cable car too. It was a moment of blissful tranquility.

After we had had our round trip, we ambled back down the steep slopes of the way we came, towards the shuttle station and back to the ship. We stopped on our descent via a plateau that offered a brilliant viewpoint over the city and port, and out to sea. There also happened to be a large kiosk, so we bought an icy cold lemon slush, complete with a straw. Yes, a straw. This was an exciting moment for me as only a week or so before leaving England, I learnt to use a straw. Now, I am the master of the straw that is both a drinking aid and a toy. The drink was delicious, by the way.

Because Barcelona's port is so big, the coach takes you across a huge bridge that feels perilously high from the raised vantage of a coach window seat. Barcelona is actually Europe's busiest cruising port. Annually, it will welcome in excess of 2.7 million passengers. In other words, that's roughly a quarter of a million people each and every month, or about 7,500 people per day. Is it any wonder that from 22 October 2023, Barcelona is limiting the number of cruise ships that can dock in its port? Instead, visitors will be sent to an alternative nearby port a thirty minute shuttle bus away from the city centre.

Once we had departed our coach in the port, we then purchased a couple of souvenirs from the Duty Free and settled back into ship-life. Daddy went to the theatre show this evening, so Mummy and I had a nighttime stroll around the promenade deck. I really had an excellent day, made all the better by the fact that we weren't victims of any crimes. What a result.

TODAY IN HISTORY

On 11th September 1297, William Wallace defeated the English at Stirling Bridge. In 2012, Andy Murray clinched his first Grand Slam title, the US Open - a month after being crowned Olympic champion.

I'm not going to expand further on todays historical offerings. I think we've had quite enough history and excitement for one day. And on that note, in the words of The Corrs, I shall bid you farewell until tomorrow comes, when we'll just do it all again.

IT'S THAT WAY

12 September

GAUDÍ GALORE, LET'S HAVE AN EXPLORE

SUNRISE 07:28
SUNSET 20:06

They say that travel enriches the mind. Whoever 'they' are, would be right as I am rich with lots of deep and topical ponderous thoughts. For example, if you're going to build a cathedral- specifically the Basílica de la Sagrada Família, why would you not curtail the design to ensure you could see it completed in your lifetime? For example, Tolstoy managed to reel in his half a million words epic that is *War and Peace* and complete that in six years. And Proust spent the final fourteen years of his life writing a 1.2 million word book called *Remembrance of Things Past*. At least they both completed these behemoth books, even if people are so put off by the astronomical length of them that they just read the blurb and economise with the truth, claiming that they've read the book. It really is a shame that we can't just ask Gaudí what he was thinking. Forty-three years after beginning work on the Sagrada Família, Gaudí went and died. Even he got bored of waiting for his grand design to materialise in its completed splendour. But, having said that- much like Arvia, the Basílica is a mammoth construction and quite something to behold- that's if you can see it through the gazillions of other tourists.

On the entrance to the cathedral (where the ticket booth is), there is a Christmas tree that is part of the building, complete with twelve doves. I imagine that this is probably quite symbolic, but we'd wondered independently away from the tour guide in search of a toilet for yours truly. No such luck: we had to have an alfresco change by a pond and some pigeons in the park. I like to keep things classy and tried to maximise my temporary and honorary membership status of the BNO (Barcelona Nudist Organisation). Full membership can only be granted once one has lost their clothes-including undergarments, on the public beach. Although- as you would expect, members of the BNO do not carry membership cards on account of the problematic conundrum of storage options. Instead, we maintain our commitment to clothes aversion by practicing the art of nakedness (not that I went totally nude today).

Forgive me, I have digressed. I am assuming that the twelve turtle doves are a representation of the twelve disciples. Which would then make Jesus the partridge in the tree. Either that, or they symbolise the twelve days before Christmas. Is that Epiphany? I for one will have an Epiphany when I find out why there's twelve turtle doves on a Christmas tree in the middle of Barcelona.

My mistake, I was the wrong side of Jesus' birthday with Epiphany. It turns out it is actually twelve days after the big day and not twelve days before. I knew the number twelve was involved, but just didn't know where. It's the time between the 25 December and the wise men arriving in Bethlehem. It turns out that the Christmas tree is on what is known as the eastern-facing Nativity Façade of the cathedral. This section is dedicated to Jesus' birth and early life. Incidentally, this is also the only façade that Gaudí watched being built during his lifetime between 1894 and 1930. Much of the rest is now posthumous.

In case you're wondering, the tree is not a pine or fir. No, it's a cypress tree. I suppose, that type of tree is more suited to the Mediterranean climes, than a Norwegian spruce. Even if it is made of stone. Fun fact: the cypress tree is the most hypoallergenic choice of Christmas tree- very thoughtful of Gaudí, I think you'll agree, as it does not produce sap. The tree also serves a dual purpose. Not only does it reflect the Nativity, it is also symbolic of the Tree of Life (even if it is more commonly depicted as a Baobab tree, as that can live for more than 500 years). Gaudí was hardly going to start following the crowd with his choice of tree, so perhaps he chose something that he liked?

The Passion Façade of the Sagrada Família.

I can't tell you what the inside of the cathedral looks like as we were on a whistle-stop tour. What I can tell you is that the outside has lots of long stringy bits on its Passion façade, which faces to the west (as shown in our picture sketch. If you look closely, behind the pillars on the right, you can see the film covering the scaffolding on the Nativity façade, flanked by a giant crane on the edge of the image. The building looks rather complete from this perspective, but that's a clever bit of image manipulation with Mumma stood at an odd angle to get the picture, thereby avoiding the perilous obstacles of both people and traffic. If it was me, I'd have used the zoom function, but my parents always seem to forget that this is an option and instead, voluntarily choose to become atrocious contortionists).

Left to interpret the wonders of the Sagrada Família, I naturally assumed that these long, narrow, vertical skeletal pillar-things were supposed to be a metaphor for tree roots and therefore a faith that is always growing. Perhaps that is why the Basílica is so tall? Or maybe not. The Passion façade is dedicated to the death and resurrection of Jesus and features sculptures showing the final few weeks of his life. Gaudí wanted this façade to look like it was made of bones, which it does. Bones from dinosaurs perhaps, as I doubt there would be any big enough animal bones- other than the whalephant. I told you travel was enriching.

Incidentally, there is a third façade to the Sagrada Família. This is called the Glory façade and faces south. It is the newest section and celebrates Jesus. Did we see this? No. We had become our own faction and branched out from the tour as I was gaining my BNO stripes, so we missed that façade.

On our coach tour, we did a drive-by along Montjuïc, stopping to circle a roundabout slowly nearby the

Hotel Mirimar. We had an aerial view of the gardens we sat in yesterday, which was nice. From the coach vantage point, we were able to confirm that this was indeed the spot where cable car number one left from. On the drive along, we then passed the starting point of cable car number two and its elusive funicular. Here was the proof that we could have saved ourselves the entrance fee of the Wet T-Shirt Competition, if we'd only walked in a straight line! Still, on the plus side, the parents had a complimentary mountain workout- a nice little holiday bonus.

Before I forget- and while I think of it, I should mention that a few nights back, we bumped into José Pizarro- the famous Spanish chef, in the lift. He was very nice and thought that I was too. A picture of him featured in one of the *Horizon* details, which was how I could identify him. In the picture, he is posing in his white chef jacket. He has a friendly face with round glasses and a substantial beard. Disappointingly, he is not wearing a huge chef hat. A couple of days later, we saw him again and Mummy asked José how his book signing went. He said that it had gone very well and that they'd sold out, so he was happy about that. I got a smile and a wave, which I duly reciprocated. Daddy was impressed that he'd recognised Mummy, but we all know that it was probably cute lil' old me with my mop of curls, roguish smile and casual leg draped over the handlebar of my pushchair, that was the point of recognition. All told, he was a thoroughly decent chap and very friendly. That said, we still didn't buy one of his books.

Around the same time, we also saw the captain walking around the ship. That was on the same day that I saw a real-life Wallace and real-life Gromit take to the stage. The captain was dressed all in white- not a smart move, if you ask me. From personal experience, I can tell you that top to toe white is not for the faint-hearted and should only be attempted if you have NO plans to consume anything red; play on grass; bottom shuffle anywhere; crawl anywhere; climb anywhere... In fact, if you're planning on doing anything when all in blanco, my advice to you is don't. The stain scenarios are just too numerous and far too risky. I find that it also exasperates Mummy, so perhaps Captain Camby could consider a navy attire instead? I'm sure his mother would be very appreciative of the gesture, because I know that mine would be.

Back to today. Our coach tour took in the main streets of Barcelona and featured famous Gaudí buildings that weren't the Sagrada Família. From what we saw, all of these were finished. They were very surrealist, but somehow drew your eye in with the soft sweeping curves of the materials and beautiful colour palette. I've got to hand it to him- the man might not have been particularly good at time management, but he sure had style.

After the Gaudí tour, we visited our favourite place on the tour: the 1929 World Expo Village. It featured 117 replica buildings of Spanish houses and constructions from across the different regions of Spain and its neighbouring Spanish islands. It was cleverly divided into four areas, representative of the different regions: the South, the Centre, the Mediterranean, and the North. Unfortunately, we had such a short time there that we weren't able to fully appreciate it all. I don't even think we were able to stand and take in the wonderment of the location, as the clock was ticking to make sure we were all back on the boat in time as the captain waits for no-one. Mummy liked the umbrella street, which is in Barcelona, I think. I could be wrong and confusing it with an umbrella street in Portugal, but the rainbow colours of the brollies hung high above the street at the Poble Espanyol (The Spanish Village) cast soft shadows and made you feel like you were the star in a Disney live animation action film. It was magical.

Mummy and Daddy liked the Andalusian section as it also reminded them of Greece, with its white-washed walls and royal blue contrasts. By this point though, I was all cultured out. I was hot and getting bothered and somewhat agitated with the constant in, out, in, out, shake it all about, in and out of the pushchair and the coach. I may as well have been doing the hokeycokey. I was never in one for long enough to make myself comfortable. So, by way of compensation for all the in, out, in, outing, I was rewarded with a strawberry ice pop. Oh my goodness, it was next level scrumptious. It was basically a Spanish Calipo. But after all the culture that I'd been absorbing, I needed a cultureless something and this was the perfect antidote. Ice cream yesterday. Fruity ice today. We really must go on holiday more often. And while we're on the subject of perishables, extra bueno news: my

116

dinner this evening was sublime. Admittedly, I was ravenous, but haddock, spinach, peas, broccoli, carrots and potato really hit the spot.

If we ever come back to Barcelona again, I would want to explore the 1929 village and its surrounding areas. These include the buildings of the Barcelona Olympics, as well as the most spectacular royal palace. A thirty minute whirlwind whizz certainly does not do it justice.

FURTHER INFORMATION ON BARCELONA

La Rambla is a street in central Barcelona. A tree lined pedestrian street, it stretches for 1.2 km connecting the Plaça de Catalunya in its centre with the Christopher Columbus Monument at Port Veil. La Rambla forms the boundary between the neighbourhoods of the Barri Gótic to the east and the El Raval to the west. Thronged with street entertainers, stalls and bars it is most lively at night and weekends. Not to be missed is the La Boqueria food market with its extraordinary displays of fish, meat, fruit and vegetables.

Rising high above the emerald green tree lined marble avenues is what can only be described as a breathtaking statue of Christopher Columbus. Interestingly, Columbus is actually Italian, but he died in Spain. He's commemorated 196 feet (60 m) into the sky, from a platform that marks the spot where he returned to after his first expedition to The Americas. The statue was built for the Barcelona World Fair of 1888 and is known as Monument a Colom (The Columbus Monument). Signor Columbus is the chap most famously credited with discovering America in 1492. Helpfully, he confidently points in the direction of Mallorca, which also happened to be in the direction of the port where the ship was docked. Yesterday, he kindly pointed us in the right direction when we were descending Montjuïc and wandering how to get back to Arvia. Daddy noticed Signor Columbus and said that all we needed to do was follow his arm. So that we did. Thanks must go to the clever bods back in the 1880s who had the foresight to install Christopher instead of the Greek goddess Athena, opting to point his hand for the sweaty, weary travellers to guide them safely back to their shuttle service and the docks. It's very impressive.

Before I finish this chapter, I must tell you something else: all of the fountains in Barcelona are dry. They have no water in. An irate local approached our tour guide when we were on foot and heading towards the Sagrada Família. They engaged in a heated discussion with lots of arm movements and sly eye gestures to us assembled tourists. The guide then explained that the locals blamed the tourists for the lack of water, which is strange because it's not exactly like you can steal water. When you see a fountain without water, it looks very odd. There is absolutely no beauty or magic- just an empty, concrete basin. If only the darn tourists didn't insist on showering, Barcelona's fountains would be in full flow.

For the next instalment of my riveting holiday journal, be sure to go for the companion book. I've not yet written it, but I assure you that it will be riveting stuff. And with that, this notebook has now run out of pages. Onwards, to tomorrow and the promise of a blank notepad. Such luxuries.

ICE CREAM OR GELATO?

13 September

FOOD FOR THOUGHT

SUNRISE 07:42
SUNSET 20:26

First up, welcome to this new book, purchased from the bric-à-brac shop built over the Roman ruins in Cartagena. I know, you're not *actually* holding a separate book, but when this was being written in the dead of night- often on the bathroom floor and by hand, a second notebook was cracked into. Mummy was going to go for a complimentary spiral bound offering to match the original journal, but then she was distracted by a pair of *Harry Potter* notepads with quotes that tickled her, wherever that may be. Perhaps the tips of her toes, or maybe the end of her nose? Who knows? The one she selected for my *Toddler on Tour Journal- Take Two,* has a quote emblazoned across the front by the inimitable Mrs Weasley: *Just because you're allowed to use magic now, does not mean you have to whip your wands out for everything.* Its notebook partner had a different thought for the day that Mummy was rather taken with: *Words are, in my not-so-humble opinion, our most inexhaustible source of magic.* That is a quote by one of Mummy's favourite literary characters- second to Aslan, the great Professor Albus Percival Wulfric Brian Dumbledore- the wisest wizard of all time, brought to life by the incomparable J.K.Rowling. Without a shadow of hesitation, Mum ditched the sensible, practical spiral offering and opted for the dangerous blank page, devoid of the stabilising presence of printed lines. What can I say? Mummy's a loose cannon.

I'm hoping that you now feel sufficiently welcomed to this new chapter. When Mummy and I purchased my original holiday notebook (now elevated in price and value since I embellished the front cover yesterday, following an unauthorised pen grab. I saw a window of opportunity and I took it. I'm not sorry. In fact, I'd desecrate one of Mummy's many notebooks again in a heartbeat. Life is for living, is it not? If Mum's the loose cannon, then I'm the ball).

As I was saying before I interrupted myself, when we bought my empty Spanish journal, we were convinced that an A5 size would be adequate enough for a fortnight. How wrong we were. It's probably a good assumption to be incorrect on, as I suppose its testament to a jolly grand holiday. This is certainly not a log about us loafing beside the pool with a cocktail to hand for fourteen days. No, most definitely not.

Because that would probably be slightly illegal as I am currently sixteen years and eight months too young for sanctioned alcohol consumption. As if by magic, I'm sure that time will just fly by.

Speaking of magic, did you know that each ship in the *P&O Cruises* fleet has a fairy godmother? Well, a godmother at least. The godmother of Arvia is Nicole Scherzinger of The Pussy Cat Dolls and television singing judge fame. I wonder what godmothering a giant ship entails? Perhaps at the stroke of midnight, if there was no official godmother, the ship would turn into a Viking longboat, exposed to the elements of the treacherous North Sea, crewed by mice with the captains uniform in tatters. And worse: communal bathrooms. Or maybe I've just leapt to an obvious answer to the question. I'm fairly certain that if there was no godmother, weird things might just happen. Which makes me think that all those ships lost at sea to Davy Jones' locker and the Bermuda Triangle evidently didn't have a godmother. I can see no other plausible explanation. Can you?

The Bermuda Triangle is a bit of a paradox. It is a highly busy area- both land and sea, and is one of the heaviest travelled shipping lanes globally. And yet, the deepest point of the Atlantic Ocean is found within the Bermuda Triangle, some terrifying 27,493 feet (8,380 m) below the surface. That is over 5 miles down. Nobody really knows how many ships or planes have been lost to the Triangle of Bermuda, but it's estimated to be about fifty ships and twenty aeroplanes. None of the remains of these missing vessels have ever been found. Perhaps that's why mariners are such a superstitious lot. There is no deck 13 on our ship. Our cabin is situated on deck 12. Directly above us is deck 14. Strange really, as the number thirteen is Mummy's lucky number. She figured that because it's so unlucky for so many, it must be lucky for someone, so she nominated herself to be said lucky someone.

TODAY IN HISTORY

On 13th September 1957, The Mousetrap, a murder-mystery, became Britain's longest running play, reaching its 1,998th performance.

FUN PARENT FACT

Fast forward to the present day, and over 28,000 performances of *The Mousetrap* have been given and over 10 million tickets have been sold- including a pair of tickets to my Mummy and Daddy when they were still in the dalliance stage of their relationship. (That's the stage before 'proper dating', when you're not quite an official couple). It was a long time ago- about twelve years ago, meaning I was lightyears away, in a far off galaxy with all the other little souls who are yet to be thought of, before being transported into Mummy's tum-tum-Tummerson when the parents do grown-up things that I don't think I need to concern myself with. Moving on.

After dinner today, we took a stroll around the promenade deck. I ventured out of the pushchair to stretch my legs, but this meant that progress was slow. However, I am a great believer about being in the right place at the right time, making everything happen for a reason. Well, tonight my philosophy was rewarded. Twice. Firstly, because my walking speed is inordinately slow, we ended up lingering on the starboard side of the ship for far longer than was strictly necessary. This turned out to be most fortuitous as we got to see some marine life in action, in the wilds of the ocean. Yes, we watched as lots and lots of dolphins passed us by, swimming freely. We even think that we saw a Mummy dolphin with her calf, as their dorsal fins were super close. It's quite special as during this trip we got to see some dolphins at the Oceanographic in Valencia. But to see this treat of nature was an unexpected moment of pure joy-especially when ten of the forty-three species of dolphin in the world are in danger of extinction. Watching them play and swim by was truly rapturous. And then, thanks to my dawdling skills, we got to see a spectacular sunset and watch as the huge copper sun slowly sank into the oceans horizon line. So there we have it: slow and steady wins the race, as foretold by Aesop's *The Tortoise and The Hare* fable, written way back in the mid-sixth century BC. So, minus six hundred from the year zero. That's over 2,500 years ago.

After breakfast, we went to the Turtle Tots. This is basically a nursery group. We'd been to a pirate one previously, which was a little underwhelming.

But todays one was jungle themed and totally brilliant because it involved three important factors: bubbles, music, and Mummy and Daddy. There was also a floaty canopy with balls. It was a little bit magical and captivated my attention for a good five minutes until I got distracted by a rogue ball and went off in pursuit of it, before Daddy rudely stopped me in my stride and deposited me beneath the rainbow canopy. It was nice to see other babes, but it was also equally nice to get to use the tambourine.

Did anything else of interest happen today? Well, actually, yes. Mummy went to a 'How to Catch a Killer' lecture. I'm not sure if she's planning on becoming a one-woman vigilante, but it seems that she's in good company as every single seat in the theatre was taken. It was standing room only. Death, is morbidly interesting it seems, to those that are living and breathing. Humans really are strange creatures.

At lunch, we left Daddy sunbathing on the balcony. Mum put me in the pushchair and I played my part of adorable baby to Oscar-worthy perfection. Mummy walked into the self-service luncheon buffet and got something for herself, something for yours truly- the greatest narrator of all time, and a salad for Daddy. With both hands on the pushchair, she was left with no choice: abandon me, or abandon the food. Only joking. The food was never in any danger. No, Mummy is smart and channelled her inner cunning criminal mastermind. After all, she'd had a crash course in how to catch a killer, meaning she'd inadvertently had a window into the criminal mind. Intentionally, Mummy had sacrificed my nappy bag in the cabin, because as she learnt earlier today, the best crimes are polished and refined and seem to happen in plain sight. This left valuable plate space in the luggage compartment of my perambulator. Oozing with confidence, Mum stashed the goods and exited the restaurant without so much as a backward glance. Yes, I was complicit as some of those perishables were intended for me. Ladies and gentlemen, I was the decoy and Mummy was my mule.

Taking a break from ray-catching, we all consumed the evidence of what is now known as The Lunch Raid. And then, Mummy and I went to listen to the cast of *Headliners* (*P&O Cruises* theatre company), discussing what life is like for them on-board and the intensive couple of months prior to boarding, following a successful audition process. A lot of fun by the sounds of it. But definitely a young persons game. It made Mummy feel good about her life choices. Maybe in a different life it might have been something she'd considered, but then the joys of Mummy-ing a Brontë and Wife-ing a Dadnad may not have happened. It's like I said earlier: things happen for a reason.

Exhausted by the exuberance of the youthful cast, I was sorely in need of a nap. I found my nap buddy and immediately, we were in business. Is there anything better than curling up on Daddy's chest and sharing a snooze? I'm learning that simple pleasures bring the greatest level of joy.

After a communal bowl of ice-cream, comprising one scoop of vanilla and one of hazelnut, we had a nice stroll around the prom-prom-prom-diddly-om-om-omenade.

Actually, I have a correction to make. We *didn't* have ice-cream. No, we had gelato. Having sampled both ice-cream and now gelato, I'm truly at a loss as to what the difference is. Frozen, creamy goodness? Check and check. Available in multiple flavours? Check and check. Tasty and delicious? Most definitely. I therefore conclude that gelato and ice-cream are exactly the same thing. The only difference is if you ask for a gelato, you instantly seem more sophisticated. It elevates your standing in life from enjoyer and consumer of frozen cream to gelato connoisseur. So with that in mind, let me rephrase my previous statement: Mummy, Daddy and I shared a vessel of gelato (there is no fancy word for tub. Beaker, container or goblet just don't pass muster when discussing gelato).

In case you are interested though, it turns out that there *is* a slight difference between gelato and ice-cream. You've probably already guessed that gelato is the Italian term for ice-cream. But the difference is a bit more scientific and involves different ratios of the main ingredients and a slower churning temperature for gelato to give it a denser texture. Incidentally, gelato favours milk over cream, which is preferred in the mixing process of ice-cream. It's probably just as well, as ice-milk doesn't quite have the same luxurious ring to it.

While we're on the topic of culinary accomplishments, I am pleased to report that my dinner was a roaring success. I had sea bass and vegetables, which I devoured so quickly it barely touched the sides. I was ravenous. A little jelly rounded off my meal nicely.

Top Of The Pop Arts: Warhol to Banksy

Join your Art Gallery Manager, Jack, as he breaks
down the icons of the pop and street art world,
stepping into the minds of the greats from
Andy Warhol to Banksy and introduces you to
Banksy's accidental apprentice, street art
phenomenon, Mr. Brainwash and find out why
he's the one all the art investors are watching.

Today, I learnt that a good investment in art is the
chap who painted the image of two young children sat
on a sagging bench seat, staring at a wall of graffiti.
They have their backs to us, so I'm unable to decipher
what they think of the layers of bright neon wall. The
artist is Mr Brainwash. He is Banksy's protégé. Already,
he has artworks that are £10,000-00 plus, which is a
lot for a piece of paper with some graffitied artwork
on it.

We stopped to admire the art on display in the
gallery on the way to dinner. Sensing easy prey, the art
gallery chap pounced on us with the speed of a
cheetah on a gazelle. Quickly, Mummy sidled to the
sidelines, leaving Daddy and me to fend off the art
vulture guy. After almost accidentally purchasing a
€4000-00 silk rug when in Rhodes, Mummy knows that
she is not to be trusted around salesmen desperate for
some easy commission. In her defence, the postage,
packaging and shipping of the rug was included in the
€4000-00 price tag. Still, with her appalling poker
face, Mum thought it wise to let me and Daddy feign

enough interest whilst letting the guy know that we weren't his meal ticket after all. We chatted politely, and then, for the second time today, my acting skills came into play.

'I'm really sorry not to be able to chat with you for longer, but this one needs her dinner,' Daddy explained apologetically. I was the 'this one', but in fairness, it could easily have been Mummy as she was quite peckish.

As if on cue, I looked at the chap with my best 'hungry baby eyes', and just like that, we were able to save ourselves £10,000-00 that we didn't actually have to spend. Thank you, I'll be available for autographs later.

Before I bid you farewell, I have just remembered something from yesterday. Whenever you get to a port, you have to pass through security- to varying levels of intensity. Although, for our cruise, we didn't need our passports as we were not leaving the European Union, so they remained safely stashed in the cabin safe. You pass through the port security when you exit the ship and then when you return.

After the coach dropped us back to the port, we dismantled the pram and fed it into the magic bad-stuff scanning machine. We then walked through the human-checker bad-stuff machine and emerged on the other side. It was reassuring to know that port security is taken so seriously after having to go through the whole palaver of stripping the pushchair for parts, unloading all our worldly wares, trading me between parents and emptying pockets. Note the sarcastic undertones.

As Daddy was holding me and Mummy was reassembling the pushchair, we watched as the man responsible for the ship and all her passengers' safety played on his phone. He was brazen like a raisin. Apparently, his WhatsApp messages were more of a priority than justifying all the faff that toddler travel entails. That said, a stern look from his lady boss saw his phone unceremoniously returned to the depths of his pocket from whence it came. I can have scant regard for rules at times, but even I copied his lady boss and gave him a withering look, but he probably just thought I had a bad case of the windies.

FLAMINGOES IN FLIGHT

14 September

EDNA ALMOST MISSED THE BOAT

SUNRISE 08:07
SUNSET 20:33

Welcome to Cadiz
Arrival: 7.00am
All aboard: 4.30pm

You cruise right into the heart of historic Cadiz.
Immediately across from the busy Avenida del
Puerto this Spanish port has a main square and
shopping area. From there, it is easy to find
your own way around this compact city.
The 18th century cathedral (El Nueva) and
the view from the top is worth the long
climb up its internal stairs.

As you can see, today, the boat docked in Cadiz. Below the *Welcome to Cadiz* title, it clearly states the arrival time of the ship in port and the time when all passengers and crew need to have reembarked by. However, every time you are in port, there always seems to be a call over the tannoy for some waifs and strays who are in holiday mode, have lost their timepieces and think that the ship will hang around waiting for them. Some people with port-side cabins enjoy watching the stragglers making a huffy-puffy dash onto the ship before the gangplank is removed.

Today, it was the turn of Edna from deck 8 and her two companions to be late and run the fate of a perilous disastrous time-destiny ending. I've no idea who Edna is, but I felt let down by her and her travel buddies because with a name like Edna, I can't help but think that she might just be old enough to know better. Anyway, sometime later the ship set sail and the dulcet tones of Mr Captain Camby filed through the air waves as he informed us that nobody had been left behind. Someone was watching out for Edna in Cadiz.

TODAY IN HISTORY

On 14th September 1891, the first penalty kick in an English League football game was taken by Heath of Wolverhampton Wanderers against Accrington.

As a non-football obsessive, I find todays historical offering neither underwhelming nor overwhelming. In fact, I'm not even whelmed. I am distinctly unmoved. So, I have taken it upon myself to find some alternative events that are a wee bit more fascinating.

A FEW MORE INTERESTING DAYS IN TODAY'S HISTORY

On 14th September 1629, the Spanish garrison surrendered to Frederick Henry-the Prince of Orange, in the Siege of 's-Hertogenbosch. Also on this day in 1939, the worlds first practical helicopter took off in Stratford, Connecticut. It was a VS-300 and designed by Igor Sikorsky. And- in recent history, on this day in 2020, supposed signs of life were reported on Venus by astronomers after they detected phosphine in the atmosphere of the planet via telescope.

Three points of note- one for each factoid.

The Prince of Orange is not actually orange. I can't even verify if he likes oranges, or the colour. That information is not available. The Orange part of his Princehood is from the principality of Orange in the Rhône Valley in France, after it passed to the House of Nassau in 1544- the Dillenburg branch of a European aristocratic dynasty. From then on in, it became known as the House of Orange-Nassau and forevermore associated with The Netherlands. Perhaps this is why the Dutch sports colours are orange?

I'm not sure if I trust helicopters yet. I've not been in one, but to my junior mind, they seem rather unaerodynamic. Plus, the nickname of 'chopper' is alarming to any of us who do not wish to follow the path of Anne Boleyn and her contemporaries. On the basis that a helicopter is a feat of impossible engineering, I have included it as homage to this extraordinary contraption.

I wondered if my eye sight would be good enough to see a whole different continent from Spain. It wasn't. So I can only assume that the astronomers who spied suspected life on Venus were using a very powerful camera in their telescope. Either that, or they've got supersonic eyesight that is able to see over 100 million kilometres away. Unless, they just had ultra powerful telescopes that they looked through, because I've seen planets in the night sky. I've no idea which ones, but I have definitely seen the yellowy hue of a full-stop sized planet in a sea of stars.

You won't believe this, but during the writing of my previous entry, I ran out of not one, but two pens. Fortunately, Mummy was prepared and able to find the contingency pens she always carries around for emergency writing situations such as this. Somewhere between my pot of dried snacks and the itinerary for the day, Mummy was able to prevent disaster and cracked open a new pen, ready to take up the mantle and serve in the line of literary duty. A major crisis was averted. It's not like she could even have asked a passing waiter for a pen loan as she would have come across as being like something of a relic of the Jurassic age. Honestly, she's really not that old, but to ask the digital users for something as archaic as a pen would be too bamboozling and warrant a lengthy explanation as to why Mummy prefers a pen and paper. You see, the waiters all use tablets to process ones orders. It's probably been deemed more efficient and less prone to errors. Still, it's interesting to learn that I can now confidently attribute my stubborn streak to Mummy and the genes that she has passed onto me. My love of naps on the other hand, has followed the paternal line.

Back to Cadiz.

Cadiz has a lot of history. Did you know that it is the oldest inhabited city in Europe? It's over 3000 years old, which- in the interests of clarity following my dinosaur related insinuations about my mother, is a lot, lot older than she is. Also, it is not pronounced Cadiz, as in 'Ka-dizz'. No, if you're trying to be a local Español or Española person, you would pronounce Cadiz as 'Kai'. That's in local, regional Andalusian dialect. But if you are trying to say Cadiz like a Spanish non-local, it would be acceptable to say 'Ka-dith', as if you're saying Cadiz with a lisp. If you want to be ultra authentically local, the Old Town of Cadiz is called Cadiz-Cadiz, pronounced as 'Kai-Kai'. For the Kai-Kai-ers, to be from the Old Town is a great honour, as our guide Magdalena told us. Her driver was called Jesus. She felt it was important to quantify that neither of them were Catholic. Ironic. Anyway, the Kai-Kai-ers want it to be known to the Kai-ers that they are an elite bunch, what with being descended from 3000 years' worth of history.

As it happens, we didn't actually get to see much of Cadiz. I tell a lie, we didn't see *any* of Cadiz or its Old Town, so I bought a postcard of what we missed. Actually, I'm being economical with the truth. We did see a very big bridge, and then we promptly drove across it. As far as bridges go, it was very nice and completed in 2015. We learnt that this bridge is bigger than the Golden Gate Bridge in Mummy's spiritual namesake of San Francesca City. Oh, hold on. I've just been corrected. It's San Francisco, after a chap and not a chapette.

We then passed through acres of giant salt plains. They were exceedingly flat and played host to flamingoes. Flamingoes aren't actually pink. The flamingoes eat the tiny keratin-rich shrimp in the salty sea water and consequently turn pink, which is quite cool.

As we were driving through said salt plains, some flamingoes took off, but we were looking the wrong way. Mummy thought she saw some flamingoes, but they could easily have been sitting ducks, or birds that looked like close cousins of the flamingo. The bus was whizzing along at a rather healthy speed and I was napping with my nap buddy, so Mummy was unable to seek verification as to what she had observed. But, in the interests of writing a more exotic journal, let's be assertive and offer an affirmative: yes, my Mummy definitely saw flamingoes flamingoing.

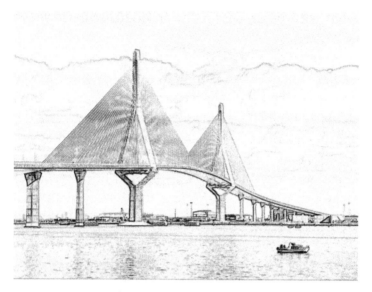

The enormous Cadiz bridge.

Our trip involved two stops- one to see a show with the famous white horses, native to Andalusia. The second stop was to a bodega, which is basically a vineyard for sherry. Both destinations were sublime- even in the 32 degree heat that I don't particularly like and that doesn't especially like me in return.

Both stops on our expedition were in the historic and very picturesque city of Jerez. From Cadiz, lots of people went on trips to explore Seville, but on account of me being such a babe, the parents didn't want to spend ninety minutes (each way) on the coach. They said it wouldn't be fair on me. That's okay: they made the right call. We'll go to Seville another time on a different adventure.

The horse school- the Fundación Real Escuela Andaluza del Arte Ecuestre, was established in 1975. It seeks to preserve the traditional equestrian dance and celebrate the horses of the region. The horses are all stallions- no mares allowed. Each year, the school accepts forty students to apprentice the professionals. The students wear green. The pro's do not. Instead, during our performance they wore dove grey and navy. Their attire was as beautiful and graceful as these mighty horses.

The school is set in jaw-droppingly beautiful grounds. There is a large central fountain (yes, in working order and complete with water cascading elegantly into the large reservoir below), a former royal palace and now a museum, as well as numerous training grounds and a purpose built arena. Stepping through the gate, there is a courtyard with orange trees. These are- of course, Seville oranges, although they should be temporarily renamed as Seville greens, for each and every orange was actually a rich, waxy, lime green. If you gently scratched the surface, the bittersweet aroma filled your hand. The guide said that there's lots of orange trees in Spain, planted in the days long before deodorant was invented. Their initial purpose was to conceal the fragrant odour of the tutti-frutti medieval folk with its delicate blossom scent.

As luck would have it, I was appropriately dressed for our trip to the Horse School. No, I wasn't wearing anything adorned with horses (although horses did feature during a rendition of Old MacDonald Had a

Farm, which was thoughtfully topical of the parents). Instead, I was bedecked with oranges. It was a two part set. The t-shirt was a pastel orange shade with two happy oranges on the front, and the shorts had oranges liberally smattered all over them. Don't tell anyone, but they're really pyjamas (have I spelt that word correctly? Pyjamas? Pjamas? Seeing both spellings together, Mummy's fairly certain that we go with the first option, incorporating the silent 'y').

Let me explain why Mumma's brain is so fuzzy. You see, I did not sleep very well last night on account of the two new teeth that I've been growing and that have erupted violently through my gums. Growing teeth is not for the faint-hearted, as I made sure to remind the parents at 1 am. Mummy also happens to be writing on the floor of our compact bathroom so that I'm in darkness and not disturbed, until the curtain screen can go up and Mummy and Daddy can finish the film that they started yesterday whilst I was in Slumbertown. When faced with the prospect of the prime bathroom seat- the throne lid, or a darkened bedroom, Daddy elected for the dark bed option, choosing to rest his eyes. Wise move.

I wouldn't usually wax lyrical about tickets to events, but as far as tickets go, the ones we were given for the Horse Show were rather fancy. They had lots of information and featured a magnificent building, which it turns out is a former palace. Everything about the school was exquisite. And everything about the eighty minute production was incredible and faultless. The performance was choreographed to Spanish classical music. I've missed hearing proper orchestral music and was verging on hypnotised, by both the visual spectacular and superb accompanying soundtrack. The first horse to arrive was a handsome lean muscular mahogany stallion, before the famed white Andalusian horses made a regal appearance.

I was mesmerised by what we saw- a truly unique spectacle where the horse and rider were operating as one. I can offer no greater accolade, other than to say that the graceful music with the flawless artistic display was indeed so awesome that I was comfortable enough to rest my eyes and siesta in the stadium. I wasn't in a deep sleep- just resting my eyes (as Mummy likes to do) and therefore able to absorb the performance by a process of audio osmosis and x-ray vision. (If you'll believe that, you'll believe anything). In my defence, it was over 30 degrees in the venue. Throw in calm, sultry Spanish music and horses and riders operating in electric silence and the recipe is just right for an afternoon catnap.

After the show had ended, we exited via a gift shop. Of course! And then, we took the short journey to the 18th century bodega in Jerez (pronounced 'Hair-ezz'). This particular sherry merchant has been in the hands of the same family for over five generations. It is almost like a living museum, except it's still operational. In the ancient days, Jerez used to be pronounced as 'Sher-ezz'. Its spelling was different too: Xerez, which is on the sherry bottle. During the reign of Queen Elizabeth I, Sir Francis Drake brought back some sherry and she loved it. And because it had the royal seal of approval, a big import-export business was established. The English traders used to call sherry 'sherrys', in an attempt at 'sher-ezz' I suppose. Until somewhere over time, the second 's' got lost and misplaced from the end of the word, until the name became known simply as 'sherry'. Four hundred years later and it looks like the name Sherry is here to stay.

At the sherry bodega, Mummy and Daddy had a tasting and tried three sherries. The first was a white, sharp, fruity floral number called Tio Pepe- the bodega's signature brew. Mummy was not a fan and promptly began devouring the tapas crackers in a bid to cleanse her palate. Daddy, on the other hand, found the Tio Pepe to be very refreshing. The next offering was called Solera and was a typical sherry colour- a burnt red. Mummy said it was scrumptious and smelt like Christmas in a cup. That was her favourite. Meanwhile, whilst the parents were a-swiling and a-sloshing, I was ensuring law and order remained from the pushchair as I nibbled some Spanish breadsticks.

The third and final taster was called something like Aperol Spritz. It was presented like a cocktail with fresh mint leaves, crushed ice, apple, elderflower and the pale sparkling sherry. Mummy declared this a triumph, which was ironic really as the Spritz was actually the Tio Pepe that Mummy had so disliked, only diluted with sparkling water. Apparently, this cocktail sherry tasted like a mojito- only better.

Whist driving through Jerez, our guide kept mentioning the Spanish medina's. I think she said they were towns, which got me thinking about home. On the Isle of Wight, there is a river called the River Medina. By island standards, she's a biggie and leads right to the heart of Newport. So, if one translates the name Medina, we have the Town River that flows into the principal town (even though the town of Ryde has a larger population. But as Ryde has the The Solent flanking her shores and no River Medina, it's not strictly relevant to this anecdote. It is merely a passing thought on the memory barge, floating up the Town River and into Newport).

Back to the bodega and its gift shop. There, Mummy and Daddy purchased a number two and number three, based on their taste test. As Mummy was queueing, a lady from our tour told her that the rumour mill was fully operational and that she'd heard you could get the number three sherry- the spritzy one, in Waitrose. Not wanting to take any chances, Mummy continued with her purchase anyway, reasoning that because it had been bought in España, it would therefore taste authentically Spanish. I know, that's flawed logic, but who's going to listen to the wisdom of a one year old?

I'd like to say that dinner this evening was a success, but unfortunately that would be a lie. On account of the two new teethies that have burst through my soft gummy gums, I had zero appetite. Not even for jelly. That's how bad the pain was. Thank goodness for the Calpol Overlords. That stuff works like a dream. When nothing else will hit the spot, go for the Calpol. That's my advice folks. And no, I'm not even working on commission.

WANTED·BIRDS
FOR VACANT NEST

15 September

WHERE ARE ALL
THE CROWS?

SUNRISE 08:21
SUNSET 20:49

We've gone wild and had a lie-in until after 8 am. You see, we are all feeling the after-effects of my teething escapades yesterday. One look out of the window though, and the overcast weather said to *take your time and relax- the sun's not due for another few hours yet.* Anyway, it appears that most of the other guests on the ship were thinking along the same lines.

Having had a gentler morning, we breakfasted around 9:30am- a lot later than usual, with every other person on board. It was slightly mayhemic.

Hmm, I don't know if that is a real word, but I'm sure you get my drift: an organised set-up, yet with undertones of mayhem and those in need of a morning dose of caffeine. To avoid the crowds, we had an alfresco breakfast, which was very pleasant.

Just behind us, on the open sun deck, there were the hardcore holidaymakers, wrapped up in towels and laid down on the prized sun loungers, confidently awaiting the arrival of the sunshine. It didn't look like fun, but their efforts were rewarded later in the morning- or at least, the efforts of those who hadn't abandoned their posts as they'd lost faith in the weather and sought out the warmer climes of indoors. I think it was a case of Holidayitis. You know exactly what I'm talking about. The infliction that we all seem to fall victim to when on holiday: 'I'm on holiday, so I will enjoy myself dammit, even if it means I risk frost bite as I wait for the weather to change, because it will change, because I'm on holiday. Dammit.'

We ourselves, were sadly not immune from Holidayitis, when we adopted the same school of thought a few days earlier and decided to force ourselves to enjoy the frosty water of the children's splash zone. As soon as that water touched our skin, we were instantly cured of our Holidayitis and able to see sense once more. But for a few short minutes, the mania of Holidayitis permeated into our brains and we were classic victims, spellbound by the lure of holiday fun, dang it, and the ridiculous belief that we would be able to withstand Arctic temperatures in our smalls.

At 11:00, Mummy went to the Simon Dinsdale 'Cold Case Investigations' speech. It was the second in a series of three. And as you might have guessed, it was about people who had long since been murdered. A bit morbid perhaps, but oh-so fascinating. If the first presentation was busy, then this was busier still. The stairways had people parked on them in absence of being able to sit in the already occupied seats. People were standing and craning their necks to hear this fella speak. Being intuitive, Mummy snuck in and sat on the floor near the front. She made sure she wasn't a fire obstacle or trip hazard, which was considerate of her.

Due to the fullness of the theatre, Daddy and I went for a walk. We relied on Mummy to relay the juicy details- which she did. Thoroughly. She took her duty very seriously and told us as much as she could recall, beginning with the cold case of Muriel Drinkwater- a twelve year old Welsh girl who was brutally murdered in 1946. This case appalled post-war Britain and was significant in that it changed some detective procedures. Unfortunately, due to the immense amount of information, Mummy couldn't remember why the case of Muriel was so poignant in the legal sense.

Sadly, the case of Muriel has never been solved. They did- years later, recover DNA of the killer, but he is probably long-since dead. However, now his DNA is in the system, if a member of his family or descendants commits a crime and has their DNA put into the system, a match could be found on the grounds of familial factors. It is really quite fascinating what can be achieved now. Although, until a descendant puts a toe out of line, the case of poor Muriel remains unsolved.

Goosebumps appeared on Mummy's arms when Simon said that he'd given this talk on the *P&O Cruises* ship, Aurora. After, an old lady came tottering up to him and thanked him for mentioning Muriel. She told him that Muriel had been her best friend. Even as I write this now, the goosebumps have returned, but this time they're on my legs.

After his seminar had concluded, Mummy the Valiant patiently waited in line to ask a question that Daddy was equally as curious about: how does a former detective become a guest speaker on cruise ships? You see, this is Mummy's longterm goal. She wants to be able to traverse the globe with Daddy and me in tow. At the moment, she's not quite sure what her subject matter is, but she's got quite a broad knowledge base. She can incorporate the piano, she can use her counselling skills and eventually, she can be a motivational speaker, which I think she'll be very good at. Sometimes, Mummy can come across as a little bit introverted and thoughtful, but when she is on the stage, she's the master of her destiny and becomes a professional with no hint of nerves. Essentially, she's one of those weirdos who actually enjoys public speaking. Daddy and I will be the tech and support teams respectively. That, we could manage.

So, how does a former detective become a guest speaker? Purely by accident. Outside of the detecting, Simon is an avid Loch Ness investigator. To help raise funds for a friends church, he agreed to give a talk on the Loch Ness Monster. It just so happened that there was a BBC producer in the audience who was equally as interested in what Simon had to say. Soon after, an agent followed and a post-retirement career of guest speaking at sea ensued. He has a roster of twelve different shows and- according to Mumma, is very good. You can tell he is used to speaking publicly and knows how to present himself very well. Even now, he seems chuffed that he gets to sail the seven seas with his wife and share his knowledge with a captive audience.

After lunch and Mummy's detailed recounting of the murder mysteries, my nap buddy and I were desperately in need of a rest. So, while we slept, Mummy went to write in a lounge up on deck 17 called 'The Crow's Nest'. She spent a glorious seventy-five minutes with a desk (coffee table strategically moved to maximise the ocean vista), overlooking the vast inky blue seas in blissful silence. She was cheered to see that of the twenty or so other people in there, they were all old-school kindred spirits and had either a pen and crossword, or a proper book with real paper pages that you can turn, with the familiar smell of printed ink. The Crow's Nest was not the draw for kindle users or WiFi phone people. It offered a momentary hiatus to the modern world and a refuge from techno goods. It was wonderful.

I'm glad that Mummy had a nice time in The Crow's Nest, but the burning question I wanted to ask was why is it called The Crow's Nest if there are no crows? Where are all the crows? And why is nobody else curious as to where our winged friends are? It must just be me. Still, using a process of logical deductions (thank you Detective Dinsdale), I am able to reason that it is called The Crow's Nest metaphorically: because it is so high up on the ship, in the forward of deck 17. When I get home, I need to ascertain if crows nests are also really high up in the trees.

If you're as intrigued as I was, you may be interested to learn that I was partly correct. Crows like to nest towards the top of a tree canopy and prefer to be higher up, hence why a crows nest on a ship is situated high-up on a mast: to give maximum visibility. The lookout- or watchmen, as he would be known in the nautical world, would nestle into a cylindrical box and search for obstacles such as whales, icebergs and mermaids. On occasion, he would also indulge in a bit of *land a-hoy!* spotting.

Excuse me while I tighten my Geek Belt another notch. Etymologists speculate that the phrase 'as the crow flies' was borne of early navigation at sea. Crows will fly in a straight and direct line, so they were supposedly kept in a cage at the top of the mast. Ergo- the crows nest. When released from their cage, they would fly in a straight line, directly to land. The ship would then set a course and follow this real-life mythical creature and hope that its straight-line trajectory avoided any icebergs, whales or mermaids. The Vikings believed that crows acted as messengers between the land of the living and the land of the dead. So if you ask me, this could complicate the navigation if they can zip between both worlds.

It may have been quieter than usual up in The Crow's Nest on account of it being a Black Tie formal night and the amount of time and dedication that dressing for said formal night entails. We haven't done either of the two formal nights as penguin suits and glamorous frocks are- according to Daddy, not compatible with toddlers. Also, as you already know, Dadnad had had a premonition of me with a flailing arm accidentally knocking a waiter carrying a tray with tomato soup that then goes down a lady in a pristine ball gown. So, we opted out of the Black Tie in favour of me having space to flail my arms without causing a disaster. Wise move parents, wise move.

Due to my two new teeth on the bottom jawline, I still didn't have much appetite. I have, however, had lots of molto bueno Calpol at the recommended intervals. That said, in addition to the teething, I think I've got the start of a pesky cold.

After dinner, we bumped into Simon and Mrs Simon at the ice cream stand. We said hello and had a nice chat. He's got a new book coming out. Mrs Simon said that I was her favourite and that she'd seen me around the ship. That was very nice and made me give her a beaming smile in return.

For the princely sum of £2-00, Mummy bought a book excitingly titled *'The Cruise'*. She said it was for market research. She and Daddy are going to have a read of it and see what they would do differently. Primarily, they would use me as a narrator. And why would you not? The world, when viewed from the eyes of a one year old, is a far more fascinating place than any grown-up could possibly imagine. After all, every day is a learning curve for me and filled with new and exciting opportunities for mischief.

Whilst exploring today, we discovered the gym. Wow- it looks top-notch, filled with all sorts of contraptions and equipment. Mummy and Daddy had a quick turn on the rowing machine and burnt seven and nine calories respectively. Impressive. Equally as impressive is how Mummy didn't drop me when the strap of her wedge shoe snapped. It was only the second outing for those shoes! But ever the pro, Mummy kept walking with me in her arms, managing to keep the shoe on her foot. What a champion.

As the day drew to a close, I vehemently resisted the need for sleep, until I eventually relented with my head plonked at the foot end of my bed. And that, ladies and gents, was my day spent at sea.

P.S.

Just a little thoughtette that's popped into my head. There were no newspapers available today. They had all sold out, which is strange really as they are complimentary. So, with that in mind, I have found some retrospective fascinating facts instead.

TODAY IN HISTORY

On 15th September 1821, the Act of Independence of Central America came into agreement when Costa Rica, El Salvador, Guatemala, Honduras and

Nicaragua declared their independence en
masse from the Spanish Empire. Also on
this day, in 1997, the domain name google.com
was registered and the world has never
been the same.

I chose these two facts for simple and humble reasons. This guide book (of sorts) is inspired by España, so the Act of Independence is conveniently topical. The Spanish Empire was rather mighty, as empires tended to be. At its peak, the Spanish Empire had control of thirty-five colonies across the globe. The only continents to remain untouched by the Spanish Empire were Antarctica and Australia. Interestingly, in the same year of 1821, Florida in the USA gained their independence from the Spanish Empire, before becoming a state in 1845. Did you know that Florida was Spanish? Likewise, Louisiana in the USA was Spanish until 1800, then became French for the next three years before being sold to the USA and given state status in 1812. History really is jolly fascinating when you scratch beneath the surface.

It's extraordinary to think that since google registered their name in 1997, this techno giant has become the head of a new Digital Global Empire (DGE). Mummy's probably visited Dr Google as much as she has her actual GP. To my juvenile human mind, it's strange to also think that I was born into a world with information readily available at the tap of a finger. And yet, before the expansion of the DGE, we were in the age of the BAF: Books Are Friends.

To prove how rapid google's online presence is, as of a study conducted in 2022, google.com was found to be the most visited website, with an astounding 89.3 billion visits to google made every month. Yes, every month. And if your mind hasn't quite been blown away, let me leave you with this parting google fact: 8.5 billion searches are made using google every single day. Yes, every single day. That equates to 99,000 searches every single second. I don't know about you, but I need to sit down to properly digest these numbers of such dizzying proportions.

CLASSIFIEDS

RELIABLE EMPTY
OAK SHELF SEEKS
NEW AND USED
BOOKS FOR SOME
COMPANIONSHIP
♡

16 September

I'VE FINALLY FOUND
MY SEA LEGS

SUNRISE 08:09
SUNSET 20:25

How's this for ironic: the day before we return home, I've finally found my sea legs. I am now thoroughly used to the gentle sway of the ship and actually find it quite comforting. So much so, I don't think I'm really ready to be land bound for the foreseeable future.

I have loved being a buccaneer of the high seas with Vice Admiral Mummy and Captain Dadnad by my side. Together, we are the three sides of a triangle. Secretly, I'm going to miss being in the same room as the parents. There can be no better start to the day than leaping to ones feet, tearing down the shower curtain wall and greeting your favourite people with a sleepy smile. I always think that it's better to have a smile to welcome a new day, once one has gotten over the shock of waking up. ABBA should rename their breakup song because- in my opinion, *waking up is never easy to do.*

I attended the final Turtle Tots nursery group today. The theme was the farmyard and it was rather good fun. It was nice to see my fellow little people and enjoy some activities at our eye level. A lot of the session involved me expressing my wanderlust and newly found independence as I liked to saunter off using my arsenal of travel skills, from walking, to crawling, to Dad's favourite- the bum shuffle. Swiftly, Mummy would stand up and chase after me. She'd then catch me and deposit me back with the group. I liked that game and kept at it for a good quarter of an hour. There's lots of things to see on a ship the size of Arvia! Plus, as you already know, I take my job of toddler *very* seriously and felt that Mummy could benefit from a bit of post-breakfast cardio. You're welcome Mumma. Anytime!

We skipped Detective Simon's third and final lecture, partly because we had to do some packing, but mostly because the theatre was full to bursting. And that was with ten minutes to go before kick-off. I don't think there was any space left for even the smallest of bottoms.

I don't know what was more popular: the charismatic detective or the draw of murder. Given that after Shakespeare, the next bestselling author is Agatha Christie- the behemoth of the crime world, I'd say that human's are innately fascinated with the subject of death. It's just not something they admit to in case people think that they're a bit weird. But once on-board a ship at sea, people happily go along to a murder chit-chat because they're in a room full of strangers, so the honorary code is to not tell on your fellow passengers and reveal that- really, you're all just as weird as each other. So you say nothing. What happens at sea stays at sea.

After we collected me some whole milk (prior to my nap of the day), we saw the captain. He rather helpfully had his hat on, so we knew it was him. Also, there's a picture of him with his bio. In the picture he is wearing a black formal jacket with four gold stripes on each shoulder and his embroidered hat. He has a well-groomed brown beard and jolly smile. Crucially, he looks like a man you can trust to steer a giant ship. The only difference between the captain that Mummy and Daddy saw on their honeymoon and now, was- just like my wonderful Dadnad, Captain Camby was a bit more salt and peppery in the facial hair department. The hat was stuck firmly to his head, so I'm unable to comment any further. Still, he was a very pleasant chap- even if he did insist on wearing risky dangerous white and treading that wobbly laundry tightrope.

Introducing Your Captain...
CAPTAIN ROBERT CAMBY

Captain Robert Camby was born in London and introduced to sea by his father who

served in the Royal Navy. At 13, he won
a music scholarship for piano and violin
to St. John's School in Surrey, which was
no surprise, as his maternal grandfather,
the late Johnny Douglas, was the highly
acclaimed film music composer of
'The Railway Children', amongst others.

He began his career at South Shields, Nautical
College as a cadet with P&O Princess Cruises
in 1995, sailing on Canberra. He gained
his masters ticket in 2003, and in 2005
he was appointed as navigator to Cunard's
Queen Mary 2, and appointed Deputy
Captain in 2008. He is a member of the
Honourable Company of Master Mariners,
The Lord's Taverners and is a Freeman of
the City of London. In December 2011
he was promoted to Captain and has
commanded Oceana, Oriana, Aurora,
Azura, Arcadia, Ventura, Queen Mary 2,
Queen Victoria, Britannia and Iona.

He is delighted to have been asked to be the
inaugural Captain of Arvia and looks forward
to welcoming you all on board. He lives in
Warwickshire with his wife Danielle and
their sons Austin and Jenson.

That's quite an act to follow up. I can't really say
much about me, the toddler on tour, other than I've
learnt to walk and am now the proud owner of eight

glorious teethies. Like the captain, I too, play the piano. I was established in 2022 and live on the Isle of Wight with my parents. They do not have first names that I know of. They are simply Mummy and Daddy.

On his walkabout, the captain looked at a semi-tired me in my pushchair and then- with a knowing smile, said to the parents that he remembered the days of pushing babes that didn't want to fall asleep. It's true: as junior members of the human race, it is our prerogative to fight the need to sleep at all times. Our greatest problem is that we all have an immense fear of missing out.

By the time that Mummy went to write in the crow-free Crow's Nest, my partner in crime and I were losing the battle of wills against the lure of sleep's clutches. It was quite a stubborn skirmish on my part, but my drooping eyelids meant I had to concede defeat and forfeit the traditional toddler right to refuse to snooze. So, we saw a nap window and we gladly took it, grasping it with open arms.

Mummy was gone for an hour or so, enjoying her sea view and being able to stare out of the window ponderously at various intervals (I think that's what writers do. Or at least, that's what they do in my mind). Given that she has spent a lot of time on the bathroom floor this holiday, writing, she revelled in the upgrade of a chair with complimentary table. The view superfluous to those two fundamental pieces of furniture.

Today, we went on a mission- out of curiosity, to find the library. Admittedly, we should probably have sought the library out sooner than the penultimate day. But a fortuitous spontaneous encounter with a member of the ship's team (beneath the importance of the captain, but with one stripe on each shoulder that said he was pretty essential to the ship's navigation), confirmed that there was in fact a library on board Arvia. That said, I use the word 'library' in the loosest possible sense. As coincidence would have it, a fellow guest sharing our lift informed us- purely by chance, that he was destined for the library. So, we followed him. Not in a stalkerish way, no. Rather in a manner where perfect strangers serendipitously meet and are bound for the same finishing point. The only difference was that he knew where he was going and we were flying blind.

Upon arrival to the 'library', we couldn't help but feel rather underwhelmed. I mean, between me, Mum and Dad, we own more books than the ships' library. And we don't have a library. We have- what we refer to as, book shelves. However, as demonstrated by *P&O Cruises*, if one employs some creative and artistic license, it transpires that anyone can own a library. All that is required is a minimum of a dozen books and you've got your very own bibliotheque. I know this to be true, because what we saw was a dozen or so tall units lined up along one long wall, obscured by doors and a voile sort of fabric, which, I can only assume was to try to conceal the bareness of the shelves. The end cupboard on the right though, was full to bursting. I didn't want to say anything, but I couldn't help but wonder why the books in that one solitary unit hadn't been distributed around some of the more naked shelves. After all, what is a library without books, if not a furniture nudist?

I wasn't actually after a book, but I would have been mightily disappointed if I'd have wanted something for the Under 3's, as this section of the library was noticeably lacking. Fortunately, Mummy had the foresight to pack me three books: my zoo lift-the-flaps number, a peek-a-boo one, and my Vivaldi Four Season's musical book. Given that she forgot to pack the music thingy from my bedroom, this last book was a superb choice.

Mummy and Daddy were a bit surprised by the literary haven being little more than a book collection point, just off a bar and parallel to a main hallway to several restaurants. From their honeymoon aboard Azura, they recalled a library reference room, complete with thick, leather-bound style books. You know the ones I mean; the sort of books that make you feel more intelligent, simply by looking at them.

The reason for the library hunt was so that Mummy and Daddy could look at a map and establish what the huge random rocks were that we saw yesterday during our alfresco breakfast. I admit, random rocks does not sound especially knowledgeable. No, it sounds distinctly amateur. At a guess, I'd say they were definitely Spanish rocks. Not because they were painted red and yellow or hosting castanet wielding flamenco dancers. No, purely because I'm assuming we were traversing Spanish waters.

Question for you: at what point does water cease to have a nationality? Is there a definitive line? From our house, we have a view over the English Channel. Does that therefore make the water on the horizon English? Or am I looking at French aqua? Or, is it in the *No Man's Land* of The Channel, neither French nor English? If someone was born at sea in a vessel in the English Channel, would they be French or English, dependent on what side of the water line they were on? Nope. It turns out that they would be citizens of the country from where the boat they were travelling on was registered. This means that if you were born aboard a ship registered in Panama in the Channel, that would make you a Panamanian, even if you'd never stepped foot in Panama. Incidentally, Panama happens to be the most popular place to register a ship.

Oh heck, it appears that the cold that has tickled the back of my nose for the last two days is more than just teething related. I believe that I have also inadvertently caught something and passed it onto my musketeer colleagues. d'Adtagnan had a bit of a headache and general face ache yesterday that has persisted. And Maramis had the telltale signs of a sore throat. Although, when she woke up this morning, the sore throat had been replaced by a headache. I guess though, when you travel- irrespective of whether you fly, cruise, road-trip, train, or any other form of transportation, the chances that you'll pick something up are immense. And let's be honest, we're on a ship with over 6000 souls on board. If the pandemic left us with at least one takeaway thought, it's this: essentially, the world is one giant petri dish.

As I clambered all over the soft play equipment and let off some steam with supervisor Daddio, Mummy did the packing of the suitcases. It's incredible how much laundry three humans can generate in a fortnight. Mummy's going to have a field day when we get home, what with all the laundering, pressing and folding. Oh hold on. Does Mummy actually enjoy doing the washing routine? She doesn't complain about it, so I just assumed it was one of her hobbies.

At teatime, we collected my blended puréed goodness, but I didn't have much of an appetite. Thanks new teethies! In the end, I was feeling so grotty that I had porridge in the cabin, followed by a bath (where I accidentally got a bit too enthusiastic on the splash front and doused Mummy), milk, and then bed. As I slept, the parents finished their film. And good news: we got a bonus hour of snooze time as the clocks have moved back an hour. You might even say we have received timepensation for the hour we mistakenly lost. Here's the evidence:

> The ship's clocks will be put back by one hour at 2.00am tomorrow morning (17 September) to GMT+1.

POST SCRIPT TO 16 SEPTEMBER

Affirmative. We all have a bug of some description and unknown origins. Apologies for any lack of clarity on what we may be harbouring, but cabin 12110's residents are all feeling rather icky. I'm afraid to report that this is more than just teething woes.

LAUNDRY REQUIRING
MY REMOVAL SKILLS

17 September

FAREWELL ARVIA. UNTIL WE MEET AGAIN

SUNRISE UNKNOWN— SOMETIME
IN THE MORNING AFTER THE DAWN
SUNSET UNKNOWN— SOMETIME
IN THE EVENING AFTER DUSK*

*   I have no idea what time the sun decided to make its appearance today. Equally, I have no clue as to when the sun decided to hand over the reins to the moon. There wasn't a newspaper to hand with this essential information. That said, even if there had been one available, I doubt we'd have had time to read it as it was departure day and there were cases everywhere. And people. Lots of them.

Today we arrived at the Southampton terminal sometime around 6 in the morning. That captain is very good at parking his boat, it must be said. I bet he has no trouble parallel parking in a postage stamp sized space. Unlike Mummy, who would rather drive past said parking spot until a). she finds a bigger space, or b). actually, there is no b). We will always enjoy a nice walk in all weathers to avoid any unnecessary parking pandemonium. (I should here add that Mummy is actually a very good driver. She just doesn't like unneeded pressure when parking. Years ago, she decided a spot of leg-stretching was good for her. And now I'm in the mix, I can strengthen the arm muscles from being in the arms of the mothership or pushed in my pram. Soon enough though, I'll be joining Mumma on these treks of hers).

Pardon the expression, but last night I slept like a baby. I awoke still feeling a bit groggy, but otherwise refreshed and ready for the long journey home. Well, that's me being economical with the truth. We only have to go about 30 miles, including jetting across The Solent. So, I guess, we have a relatively short return journey home compared to the people who will be traversing the length of the country. How do I know this? Because there were lots of people on board who had a 'travel off'. I don't think it was a very good competition. The aim of the 'travel off' was to see if you had travelled further to get to Southampton than the person next to you. It led to some hearty debates. It's not often I'm glad that words haven't bequeathed me with their presence yet, but being silent excused me from participating in this game we were destined never to win.

After our final Arvia breakfast, we picked up our remaining hand luggage, sat in the impressive atrium for the first time all holiday, and then returned to Blighty with the familiar sight of her drizzling rain, serenading us off the ship. Connecting the ship to land (apart from lots of ropes and mechanical things) is an airbridge. Essentially, its rows of gently sloping corridors that lead you in a zig-zag down to ground level.

As we zigged and zagged to further away from our holiday and the ship, reality beckoned with the planting of our feet on terra firma. I felt slightly sad as our adventure was officially over. And then I caught sight of the myriad of different suitcases and suddenly felt very grateful that I was safely ensconced in my pushchair. Holy guacamole, it's a gauntlet of multi-coloured obstacles as far as the eye can see. With that in mind, Mumma and I nominated Daddy to venture into the thousands of standing bags and cases in pursuit of our luggage. Five minutes later, he emerged victorious.

The terminal at Southampton is quite sizeable. After being reunited with our luggage (bravo Dadnad), Mummy, Daddy and I joined the taxi queue. It wasn't moving. A land-bound terminal worker informed us the taxi wait would be very long as four cruise ships-including ours, had all docked to deposit their holidaymakers. In addition, it was also the Southampton Boat Show. So, d'Adtagnan made an executive decision:

we would walk to the Red Jet terminal. It took no more than ten minutes. Where Mummy seeks out an easy parking space and subsequent walk, Daddy seeks out lines that are moving. And as the taxi queue doubled back on itself and remained resolutely frozen, Daddy decided that- in this scenario, leggy-peggy's were better than wheels and motor power. As such, we boarded the 10:20, instead of having to wait until 11:30.

When we left The Solent and Cowes to get to Southampton on the third of the month, there were five ships docked and the *Red Jet* was stuffed to the rafters. So it was quite pleasant to have room to breathe as the return boat was virtually empty. Having said that, the queue to board the *Red Jet* to get to Southampton when we arrived back on the island, was so substantial it went all the way to the end of the gangway, through the ticket office and beyond the shops outside. As with a fortnight previously, there was an Isle of Wight mass exodus.

Grandpa met us on the other side after we left the Mainland. He then drove us to the supermarket for a few groceries, and dropped us back home after. Swiftly, Mummy set about sorting the laundry. She managed to do three loads and tumble dry two batches. What a pro. I even helped by keeping out of the way as sometimes, my efforts to help are perceived as a hindrance. I can't possibly think why, when all I am doing is commandeering clothing items from the pile and taking them on a journey around the house before they are locked in their watery tomb and their clothing memory is wiped clean. After the wash cycle is complete, I then like to unpeg all the things that Mum has hung up because pegs are more fun than most of my other toys. However, I must have reached a stage of toddlerturity as I thought that due to the volume of laundry (of which, a fair amount was generated by me), I'd keep a low profile.

Folks, it is with a heavy heart that I must share the sad news that we have had a victim of the return journey. Poor *Shaun the Sheep* is blinded in one eye, having lost the sight somewhere in transit between The Solent and home. Worse still, he has been impaled by his own leg and is now sporting the end of a cocktail stick dowel, sticking out of his back. And double worse- he no longer wants to stand up and keeps toppling onto his one-eyed face. This is a tragedy of unexpected levels. Mummy tried to conceal the horror that was Shaun's disfigured body as she didn't want me to have nightmares. She even considered allowing him to peacefully slip away via the black bin bag. But my hero, my partner in crime and my champion nap buddy Dadnad, popped his glasses onto his face, carefully held Shaun aloft and came to the rescue.

My Daddy is going to perform a complex bit of plastic surgery on Shaun's eye- well, his remaining one. It involves splitting his current eye and making a new one, so there will once again be a pair. There'll both then be grafted back onto his face. Dad's warned me that Shaun will probably look a little different, but if it saves him, we'll take that. Daddy also plans to recast Shaun's impaled leg and rebalance his hooves so that the poor lamb can stand once again. Thank goodness Dadnad's such a world-renowned plasticine surgeon, as otherwise, this episode could have had a most unfortunate ending. Following his surgery, Shaun will be most welcome to recuperate on my shelf and become my newly promoted bedroom mascot.

I forgot to put this in yesterday's entry, so here is the slice of history for 16 September.

TODAY IN [YESTERDAY'S] HISTORY

On September 16, 1387, the future
Henry V of England was born in Monmouth
Castle in Wales. In 1620, the 101 Pilgrim Fathers
set sail from Plymouth in the Mayflower,
captained by Myles Standish.

Unusually for me, I don't have much to say about the historical offering, apart from 1387 was a jolly long time ago. What you may be interested to know is that the Mayflower is highly relevant to this chapter, as there is a Mayflower Cruise Terminal in Southampton and the Mayflower Theatre- also in Southampton. If the Mayflower ship set sail from Plymouth, why is such a large theatre along the south coast in Southampton named after said ship? Well, it turns out that the Mayflower made three attempts to depart England. The first of these efforts was made in Southampton on 5 August 1620. They tried again a little over two weeks later from Dartmouth, before successfully leaving the shores of England from Plymouth in 1620. And the rest- as they say, is history.

YOUR DISEMBARKATION ARRANGEMENTS

Please meet in the following venue for your disembarkation:

Casino & Brodie's (Deck 7) Forward - 10:15 to 10:25

The approximate time you will be called from the venue to disembark will be:
10:15 to 10:25

Want to disembark earlier?
If you can carry your own luggage, then you can disembark Arvia between 6:30am and 8:00am. Just make your way to the airbridges which will be situated on deck 6 Atrium with your luggage. There is no need to register for this option and you may disregard the instructions on the front of this flyer giving you a specific time and venue for your disembarkation.

This excerpt from the disembarkation letter is quite clear. We should really start reading things currentspectively, as opposed to after. It turns out that we were supposed to have vacated the cabin by 8am. Fortunately, although slightly later, our cabin stewards didn't mind- probably because they'd become my friends. A smile goes a mile.

Not knowing what to do with them, I stuck our individual cruise cards into my journal when we got home. It felt a little bit sacrilegious to simply dispose of them in the rubbish bin. That said, I am following in my parents footsteps. There is a drawer that I know of in the kitchen which features an array of useless and pointless items which are kept- on the off chance, that one day, they might just be needed. Somewhere amongst the random contents are a good half a dozen spare keys that don't actually fit into any of the windows or the doors of our house. Who knows where they came from, or what they're for. But they're there. So, the precedent has been set. On the 'just in case' basis, I have kept our cruise cards.

Oh heck, it appears that our cold is a little bit more than a cold. As other Nanna is a bit fragile at the moment, we didn't want to accidentally gift her with our bug. She asked if we had Covid. We didn't think so, but said we'd test anyway as we had a couple of spare Covid tests (still in date). Promptly, two lines appeared on both d'Adtagnan and Maramis's tests, confirming that they were harbouring the virus. I've probably got it too, but Mummy spared me the nose delving, for which I am grateful.

We thought we'd emerged unscathed, but no. Somewhere along the way, The Covid saw a chink in our armour and snuck in in the dead of night. I suspect that I may have been the one who welcomed it into the cabin 12110 fold. Due to my issues with my teeth erupting into my mouth, I think my immune system must have been compromised. This meant that if

I caught anything, it was inevitable that my musketeer colleagues would be unable to remain unscathed and lurgy free, due to our sleeping quarters being so compact. Still, given that none of us have previously had The Covid, we're hopeful it'll just be a gentle bout and jog on its merry way as quickly as possible.

In the evening, I had a delicious dinner of steamed fish, peas, potato and broccoli, followed by grapes. It was like a wonderful palette cleanser. And after dinner, we think we saw Arvia cruising by our house. She was on the horizon line of The Channel, lit up like a twinkly beacon and overtaking a slower ploddy ship with orange lights.

All in all, I'm quite happy to be home. I will miss the adventure and waking up somewhere different each day. But, I've got my musketeers and we'll find the adventure in every day, because that's what we do. I will say; I do miss the carpet on the ship. As someone new to this walking lark, wooden floors are a lot less forgiving. However, I'm back in my own bed, which is lovely. I did grow accustomed to my travel resting space, but coming home to your own familiar things is very soothing. Can there by anything more magical than returning to fresh sheets on your bed? I guess we've got to go away to appreciate these small, glorious pleasures.

18 September

RAIN, RAIN, GO AWAY

Today is what I shall refer to as our first real 'home day', post holiday. I'm doing lots of first rate tottering all over the place, but I am missing the gentle sway of the boat. Consequently, I find I'm compensating for being on land that is rather sturdy and resolutely still by subliminally swaying from the knees up and from side to side. That feels normal, which is probably rather ironic. I don't suppose there are many people who begin their walking careers- quite literally, at sea. I'm curious to see when- or if, I stop swaying whilst standing. Probably not. Even now, I witness Mummy swaying absent-mindedly from side to side. It must be like a muscle memory. She was so used to rocking me when I was new to the world, that she still goes through the same motions on a subconscious level. Word on the grapevine is that The Mum Sway is a fairly standard thing after having a babe, so that's good. I wonder if The Toddler Sway is something my peers have too, or if it is just me? My finger is resting on my lip as I thoughtfully ponder this.

In other news, *Shaun the Sheep* is still waiting in the pre-surgery assessment office. His wayward eye is long gone, so the slice and dice surgery is definitely the way forward.

Since we've been back, the Mothership has done a further two more washes and- due to the recent abrupt abdication of the sun, the weather partners have sent us perpetual rain in protest since we returned to Inglaterra. The washing line is redundant in favour of the tumble dryer at the moment. I miss the sunshine. Not the midday one, but the less intense one that warms your cheeks and makes your hair all shiny. Somehow, the world just seems so much more brighter when the sun is out.

The absence of sunshine has probably not helped matters on The Covid front either as we all feel rather grotty, what with the post-holiday blues taking root. That said, I seem to be bouncing back more quickly than the parents. Speaking of which, with all this washing, tumbling, ironing, pressing and folding, I believe that Maramis has officially become her mother. Yep, my Mum is now a professional Mummy with the same credentials as her own Mumma. The next thing you know, Mummy will soon be graduating to Adult Cleaning. That's the cleaning where you actually pick things up and move them, instead of just going around items that are in the way. It's a more thorough process, but it's also a lot more time consuming. And given that one of my numerous hobbies involves emptying toys onto the floor, on top of general tidying, Adult Cleaning (also known as Advanced Level Cleaning), can eat into precious playing time.

Do you remember our first proper day aboard Arvia? It was the fourth of September, when we woke up and realised that we'd missed the clock change. That day. Well, I found evidence to support a prior clock change warning:

The ship's clock will be put forward by one hour at 2.00am tomorrow morning (4 September) to GMT+2.

Given that our cases didn't arrive until later in the evening and we had lots to unpack, to have a relaxing read of the *Horizon* guide, was not high up on our agenda. Still, at least we would have known to skip the hour if we hadn't been so knackered.

In the similar spirit of a bit of good old fashioned retrospectivity, I've kept the nursery itinerary to see what I missed out on. It even features details of a night nursery, whereby parents can deposit their offspring and do grown-up things like drink wine without a toddler watching curiously and attempting to taste it, or go to a show. We didn't use the night nursery as there was no way I'd have arrived asleep and stayed asleep at 6 or 7 pm. I don't even do that at home, so why would I do something like that when I'm on holiday? I'm not a robot. I'm a ~~baby~~ toddler.

The girls who worked at the nursery all seemed very nice. I didn't see any chaps who worked there though, which is funny really as- when I visited, at least 50% of the other babes and toddlers that I met were boys. It seems Beyoncé was right: girls do in fact run the world. Well, nursery's, at least.

I've also got a bit of bonus information that we kept on Valencia (since we only saw things that breathed under water and striking contemporary buildings); our boarding passes, dining and drinks info (because it's interesting to see where we could have visited), and the very serious sounding final On Board Account Statement.

According to our *Horizon* pamphlet, there is lots to see and do in Valencia. Seems as we only saw a small fraction of it, here's some info on the Old Town, beaches and waterfront.

OLD TOWN

The old town is a 30 minute walk from the shuttle bus drop off point at City of Arts & Sciences. Taxis are available from here with a journey time of around 10 minutes. Alternatively, you can get a taxi from the ship directly to the Old Town with a journey time of around 25 minutes and approximately costing €20-00.

Sorry, that wasn't quite as interesting as I thought it would be. Unless you're reading this in the year 2050, in which case it will probably be very interesting.

WATERFRONT AND BEACHES

From the port entrance you can visit the
local waterfront featuring many
restaurants and bars, explore the remains
of the Valencia Street Circuit or take a
short walk to the local beaches.

A limited free shuttle bus service will
be in operation between Arvia and the
port entrance (Transmed-Grimaldi).
The transfer time is approximately 10 minutes
each way and is subject to local traffic
conditions on the day. You could also walk
from the ship to the Transmed-Grimaldi in
approximately 40 minutes.

At this point in the original bathroom floor journal, I
thought it would be a good idea to affix our boarding
passes. These are no longer fancy, glossy things. No,
they are folded and crumpled, having been printed at
home in black-and-white on non-luxurious flimsy
matte paper. A travel agent may have glammed them
up, but in the interests of convenience, Mummy cut
the middle person out and did the printing instead.

Only now that we are home, did we notice that our
boarding passes are clearly stamped with a stamp that
reads OK to Board. What would it have said if we
weren't ok to board? And more to the point, what does
the word 'ok' actually mean? For a travel document
stamp, is it really formal enough?

A little bit of research tells me that 'ok' is actually an abbreviation for 'oll korrect', which is an intentional misspelling of 'all correct'. This was in 23 March 1839's publication of *The Boston Morning Post*. Those crazy kids certainly knew how to have fun back in the 1830s. Fast forward almost two hundred years and these misspelling anarchists have certainly had the last laugh, etymologically speaking. I think that they may just be my new heroes. I mean, I make up new words all the time. More importantly, I also speak fluent and coherent gibberish, so the folk at *The Boston Morning Post* could be onto something.

Just like our boarding passes, the dining and drinks guide that I kept for prosperity is also folded up on a crumpled sheet of paper. There really was an abundance of places to dine at- something for every palate. Firm favourites of the Musketeer Gang included The Quays and the Horizon restaurants. This was not because these places necessarily served the best or most gourmet food, but for us, these two places took the culinary crown on the basis that we could generally always find a nice, quiet spot to enjoy our dinner.

Our final On Board Account Statement makes for a rather boring, yet comprehensive list, of our spending whilst onboard. It makes Mummy and Daddy look like creatures of habit as the same destinations frequently crop up. We had £480-00 of on-board spending for our cabin across the fortnight. All I can say is it's just as well Mummy had her hair treatment and purchased the shampoo elixir and conditioner worth its weight in gold, as otherwise we'd still be in credit. So thank you Oasis spa services.

By the time we near the end of page two of the statement, the onboard credit ceases and any further spending switches to a pre-registered card. Excluding the flamboyant cost of the Bingo tickets at the start of the holiday, we spent the princely sum of £15-10 on top of our on-board credit. Because the parents had cruised with *P&O Cruises* (before I came along) for more than fifteen nights, they automatically became members of the Peninsular Club. This is basically like a reward for your loyalty. Currently, the parents are part of the Pacific tier. One of the perks of being a Pacific tier member is that once you enter into the realms of spending *your* money (as opposed to on-board credit), you receive a 5% discount on your purchases. Well, thank goodness we're members of the Pacific tier. That 79p loyalty discount will go a long way to ensuring our repeat, return business.

19 September

YES, IT'S STILL RAINING

What more can I say? It's very wet and England seems sad that we have returned from our holiday. Perhaps the world is trying to give us a hint that we need to explore more? Either that, or it's just one huge coincidence.

We're all still feeling rather yucky. This bug sticks better than superglue. It's very disheartening, having had a holiday and then, instead of feeling bright and refreshed, you feel rotten. It's not very fair at all.

The most exciting thing to happen today in The House of Plague, was Mummy doing some ironing whilst I had a nap. She also had a telephone counselling session with her new client. I supervised Daddy with smiles and games whilst Mumma did her Mum Stuff.

20 September

IT DOESN'T JUST
RAIN, IT POURS

That's right, the rain seems to be even bigger than yesterday. It's very annoying as I'm not allowed to play outside in case I catch a cold. But, on account of already having a cold, I think I must have immunity. The parents, on the other hand, think otherwise.

Do you remember the little owl that I adopted and rescued whilst on-board? Well, she's officially a member of the family now. I got her paperwork in order and now have a Birth Certificate for her. On this certificate, it has my name- Brontë, as Henrietta's new best friend; Henrietta's name, and her place of birth, which is listed as Arvia: Mediterranean Sea. I can't be sure of a precise location so have applied what I believe to be common sense. Place of birth should really be substituted with place of rescue, if you ask me. Rounding off her official certification is her birthday, which is the day she joined our clan.

27 September

WHERE ARE ALL THE POSTCARDS?

In case you're still wondering, yes, it is still raining with gusto. Nature is not doing things by halves at the moment.

Every day, I'm walking more and crawling and shuffling less. Although, as I mentioned the other day, I am still swaying. Perhaps I'm therefore destined for an ocean bound career when I grow-up as my legs are resolute and wobble free when the sea nudges the boat. Or, maybe I just need to keep practicing on land? With confidence comes stability. And with stability comes expectation.

You'll be pleased to read that I'm becoming re-accustomed to life at home and am enjoying having all my toys around me. Funnily enough (and this is something I never thought I'd say, but) I even missed my car seat. When it spent a few days in the hallway during the elective quarantine, I greatly enjoyed being able to clamber in and out of it. I guess, when I'm in my car seat in the car, that's because we're off on a quest or an adventure. And if I've learnt anything in these last few weeks, it's that I do quite like a good adventure.

Great news: Daddy's just taken another Covid test and he's still positive. He doesn't seem too happy about it though, which is strange really, because positive generally means something good. It's like a big metaphorical green tick, or a cosy victory hug. Unless I'm misunderstanding the context of the word 'positive' here. And let's face it, that is a very real possibility as I'm only sixteen months, after all.

Shaun the Sheep has taken up his new post and is now standing sentinel in my bedroom, surveying the world from on top of my Beatrix Potter book collection. I'm pleased to report that his surgery went well and (don't tell him), but he actually looks better than he did before the plasticine surgeon set to work. It really does feel very nice to have my mascot back in business and a happy memento of our Spanish Sojourn.

A question that has been niggling me for quite some time: Where are all the postcards? Nobody has received anything. I'm rather disappointed. I genuinely thought that at least one of the seven would have arrived by now. I didn't know that the Spanish post was so sluggish. Are the postcards siseta-ing, or something? Is there a postcard nap buddy, employed by the Spanish postal services to keep the postcards company before they leave for pastures new?

I'm putting on my detective hat as I ask myself if my postcards actually left the ship. The £16-10 postal service charge would suggest that yes, they said *adios amigo!*, but the empty letterboxes would suggest otherwise. I get why people call this sort of communication 'snail mail' and can totally understand why people choose to email instead of posting. Still, I was hoping to bring a smile the old-school way. I'd told an amusing tale from our time at Santiago de Compostela about how we'd basically been kicked out. It was rather chucklesome if I don't say so myself, so I shall live in hope that my masterpieces reach their intended recipients sooner rather than later.

A LEECH IN DISGUISE

22 September

CAN I OFFER YOU A PET LEECH? IT'S FREE

Good news. Both Mummy and I have recuperated and are feeling a lot better. Dad's still feeling rotten, but I suppose we all fight bugs in the same way, but differently. Nevertheless, it's good to have one of my playmates back.

Mummy might not be sneezing anymore or as tired (although tiredness is a symptom of parenthood, I've heard), but her overactive imagination has remained precisely that: overactive. She was helping me to dress and suddenly leapt back in alarm as there was a big, juicy leech attached to my tummy. Or at least that's what Mumma thought.

I'm not sure how- or where, I would have procured a leech from, but that wasn't on Mummy's mind. Likewise, I don't know why Mummy thought I would provide asylum to a leech on my tum-tum-Tummerson. Bravely, she stepped towards me to investigate my uninvited guest. A sizeable sigh of relief caused Mummy's shoulders to deflate and land somewhere near her knees. It wasn't a leech after all. It was a partially chewed black grape that had fallen down my vest. These things happen. What can I say? Hand-eye coordination is a skill that I am slowly mastering. But as we all know, good things come to those who wait.

05 November

TYING UP LOOSE ENDS

As I write to you today for my final entry in this travelogue, I have reached the dizzying heights of precisely eighteen months of life. I'm now comfortable on my feet as a walker and confident running away when I find some treasure that I would like to keep. Favourite treasures include Mummy's watch, telephones, Mummy's purse (and its contents), Mummy's handbag, the remote control and, the toilet brush. All these prizes are of the same value to me. It's just great fun to play hide the treasure. I'm good at that game. Before we went away, I hid a couple of cards that I found in Mummy's purse in a plant pot. It took her a week to find them. I'm also enjoying being able to read my books and experiment with my musical instruments. The other day, I generously hid my recorder in Mummy's handbag, because that's how much I love her. As a professional toddler, it is my duty to cause mischief and I have pledged to the Toddler Forefathers to uphold my responsibilities to the best of my ability. Considering the parents refer to me as the Mischief Maker in Chief, I'd say that I'm doing a pretty grand job. I'm very proud.

My teeth are coming through in their droves. If I thought that my teething woes on board were bad, I had to reassess my definition of the word 'bad' when six started coming through at once a couple of weeks ago. Cheese and crackers. That was horrendously bad. Now though, I'm over the worst of it and very much enjoying my ever broadening culinary choices.

I've been seeking extra cuddles from the parents this week. I'm homesick for their bedroom and our tiny cabin aboard Arvia. If I can see them, then I know that they're there. Their presence is very reassuring.

In the interests of tying up loose ends, you may well be asking yourself if the postcards ever arrived. Are you as invested as we have been in their progress? Prepare for a riveting response.

A friend and her husband went on a cruise whilst we were on our cruise. They went to Spain and Portugal and set sail from Southampton when we were halfway through our trip. They got back home a few days after we did. They kindly sent us a postcard from their holiday and it arrived on our doorstep with a happy plop on the second of October. Mummy messaged to say thank you. Curiosity got the better of her and she enquired if they had received our postcard. The answer was no. That was until we were notified ten days later to say that our postcard had indeed found its way to their house in Northwood on the Isle of Wight.

Over the course of the following week, four more postcards arrived at their Isle of Wight destinations; one to Scotland, and the other to recipients in Brighton. Interestingly, the first postcard to arrive on the island was to our Northwood companions who had received their postcard on the twelfth. On the eighteenth of October, our final postcard arrived to our friends on the island in Sandown. These friends of ours live about thirteen miles apart. Somewhere during transit, our postcard to Northwood was put onto the premium business class flight, whilst our postcard to Sandown was strapped to a hardy pigeon and sent out into the elements.

*

I'm not quite sure how to say goodbye to you. We've shared quite a journey together and I have so enjoyed being able to experience so many new things with Mummy and Daddy. Truthfully, it wasn't always plain sailing and- if I'm honest, the ship was probably a bit big for my maiden travel voyage. But, I've learnt for next time. I now know that the three musketeers can manage perfectly well in the one room (although I did already know that as I spent my first year camping in the parents' bedroom). I know that we don't need lots of stuff to have a good time and I have learnt that if I am with Mummy, Daddy, or both of them, I don't have to be afraid of the unknown because I'm with my Mumma and my Dadnad.

I loved the warmth of Spain and its people, the passion for their food, their heritage, and their history. I also enjoyed being able to walk up and down the super long corridors that take you to your cabins. They made ideal training roads for me. Most of all, I enjoyed being able to have an adventure with my musketeers.

So, until next time, dear Reader. Thank you for your company on this Spanish odyssey. It's been a blast. Who knows what the future may bring? Today, in the here and now, I'm just going to simply be, and enjoy every little twist and turn that life throws my way. Daily living may not be quite as exotic as our holiday, but it's still got a smattering of magic to it, because each day is the opportunity for a fresh start and the chance to discover something extraordinary.

A POSTSCRIPT Q&A

Before I definitely bid you a fond farewell, I thought I would answer some of the musings that you most likely have. I'll start with an easy point of pontification: am I a real person, or am I a figment of the Mumma imagination? I've just pinched myself on the arm and can answer in the affirmative. Yes, I am indeed real.

As a toddler, I had to have my passport organised when I was a bambino. This leads to the question: did I look like my passport photograph when we embarked on our adventure? No, not really. Truthfully, I look more like a baby convict. It's really not my finest depiction. But, in my defence, I had to lie down under industrial strength spotlights so no random bits of Mummy or Dadnad appeared in the picture or any peculiar shadows. The rules that HMRC have are quite strict. If you try to follow them precisely, it leads to two miserable photo shoots before the parents resign themselves to the best image of a bad bunch and simply make do, contenting themselves with the knowledge that it will need to be renewed within five years. All I can say is that- based on my passport, I wouldn't want to mess with me.

Here's a few other questions and answers of note that I thought you might appreciate.

What advice would you give to other toddlers travelling with parents?

Well, firstly, I would say to be patient with them. Parents get tired very easily, so this can sometimes make them a bit cranky. They need their rest, so use that time to your advantage. You know- delve into the Mummy's handbag, hide the remote control (after you've changed the subtitles to Spanish, because that will really flummox them), consume as many of the secret biscuit bribe stash that the parents think you don't know about but you actually do; redecorate the place by evicting everything from your travel cot and scattering it far and wide. In short, use the parent's rest time for honing your Toddler Antics Skills. And of course, now is the best time to plot your Toddlerdomination, for when you're ready to take on the world.

Travelling with parents is not for the faint of heart. They take a lot of supervision, but smile generously and make them laugh, and you'll have a blast.

Based on your experience of travelling with parents in Toddler on Tour: Viva España, would you do it again?

Yes, of course. It would have to be with my parents though, as otherwise that would be a bit odd if I randomly selected someone else's parents. That said, in all honesty, the parents do make for excellent travel companions. They also happen to be the custodians of the funds. Being a toddler, I don't yet have clearance to authorise payments of any kind. So, it's prudent to keep on the good side of the parents as they hold the purse strings and- in my experience, purse strings lead to ice-cream.

Where would you like to visit and why?

The world is a very big place, so I've kept two of my three prospective trips to the UK and the third within Europe.

At some point, I'd like to go West to Devon and Cornwall, because who wouldn't want to see a wall of corn? There, I'd detour via Dozmary Pool on my mission to retrieve Excalibur and imbue myself with magical powers and the ability to be undefeated in battle. Not that I'm planning on going into battle anytime soon. Although, what with my current passport and the sword of King Arthur, I would be a fearsome opponent. The only flaw in this plan is that many people speculate that Excalibur is actually in Wales in a lake in Snowdonia. And in case you didn't already know, Wales *isn't* in Cornwall. It's a whole other country, which would mean a totally different excursion. Given that there's millions and millions of people in the world, I'm surprised that nobody has found King Arthur's sword yet. Unless, someone *has* found it in secret and wants us to think that it's still missing. That's what I would do.

I would also like to head North. Keeping with England for now, I will undertake what I am referring to as 'The Brontë Literary Trail'. We'd stop at Haworth in Yorkshire- home of the Brontë sisters and my spiritual namesake. Once I have purchased as much Brontë memorabilia (with my name on it) that I can brandish, we will then head to the Lake District and the realms of Beatrix Potter. Her books share a shelf with my *Shaun the Sheep* mascot, so it would be nice to see the inspiration behind these well-known tales. Plus, it will get me bonus Mumma points, because Beatrix is her kindred writer inspiration. For bonus Dadnad points, we'd then head East to the coast and stop by Whitby Abbey, home of Bram Stoker's *Dracula*, as Daddy is also partial to stories that are inspired by real places. Mr Stoker is believed to have visited Whitby in 1890. It must have left a lasting impression as *Dracula* was published soon after in 1897. As we learnt on our cruise, people are secretly fascinated with the macabre. Perhaps that might explain why *Dracula* has never been out of print since it was first published.

Further afield, I would like to voyage into the lands of Norse mythology and sail through the Fjords. With waters of glassy infinite depths, mighty God's like

Thor who gave his name to Thursday (a pretty good day of the week if you ask me); the imaginatively titled Viking long boats that are essentially boats that are long; arguably the world's most beautiful and scenic railway journey in Flåm, and much more. I think Norway would be quite cool- in both the literal and metaphoric sense of the word.

Lastly, did the Brontë Mumma really write this travelogue on the bathroom floor?

Yes. Dadnad took a snap of Mumma. She was so engrossed in writing that she didn't even notice him surreptitiously peeping through the doorway. In case you don't believe me, I've included the evidence.

The Brontë Mumma.

So, that's that. It is here that I shall bid you Godspeed. Happy adventuring, my friend. And to those of you travelling with parents, good luck.

SOME WORDS
OF THANKS

Hi there, it's me, the Brontë Mumma.

I have a few thanks that I would like to make.

Firstly, as a collective, I would like to thank my husband and daughter as- without them, this book would not have been a possibility. Yes, I could have gone on this adventure and most likely had a super time without them, although that would have felt very empty to me. Would I have made the memories and had the experiences that I did if I had been a solo traveller? Most likely not. I do feely fairly certain- however, that if it had been a Mumma Mission without my husband and daughter, I would have been given the chance to have at least eight glorious hours of uninterrupted sleep each night. That, dear Reader, is the stuff of dreams. Literally. Over a course of fourteen nights, I'd have been looking at about 112 hours of time spent in the Land of Nod. But the occasional yawn was worth the time I got to spend with my favourite people.

A solo thank you to my husband for believing in my writing and me when I'd lost my way. Thank you also for your editorial assistance and guidance in the creation of *Toddler on Tour: Viva España*.

Thank you to my daughter. Being your Mumma is an exhausting, humbling and joyful experience, made all the better by the fact that your smile and zest for life makes it all worthwhile. You have magic in your spirit.

Thank you to all the wonderful people that we had the opportunity to meet on this adventure. From one day to the next, never quite knowing who we would bump into made everything so much more interesting.

And last but by no means least, thank you to you, our travel companion and reader extraordinaire. You could have chosen any book out there, but you decided to share our journey, for which I am truly grateful. I hope you enjoyed it as much as we have. Thanks for coming on tour with us. See you again soon in *Toddler on Tour: Moving Fjord*.

REFERENCES

If any of the interesting facts or little nuggets of surprising information have caught your attention and you would like to conduct a bit of your own research, the below list comprises the main sources used in the research process of *Toddler on Tour: Viva España* (listed alphabetically for ease of reference). Of course, a trip to the library is always wholly recommended. But, if you're after an instant reconnaissance at the tap of a finger, any good search engine is your go to. Beyond that, feel free to explore the wonderful pool of information that we were able to delve into.

The *Britain Today* newspaper offered by *P&O Cruises* was courtesy of KVH Media Group and the NEWSlink service. The details garnered from the *Horizon* newsletter were courtesy of *P&O Cruises*. Please do remember that this list is not an exhaustive one, but is as thorough as I can make it.

A-Z Animals - a-z-animals.com
Barcelona.com - www.barcelona.com
Barcelona Hacks - barcelonahacks.com
Barcelona Metropolitan - www.barcelona-metropolitan.com
Barcelona Tourist Guide - www.barcelona-tourist-guide.com
Barcelona Turisme - www.barcelonaturisme.com

Barcelonando - barcelonando.com

Britannica - www.britannica.com

Catalan News - www.catalannews.com

Cititravel DMC Spain & Portugal - www.cititraveldmc.com

Cultural Survival - www.culturalsurvival.org

Disabled Accessible Travel - www.disabledaccessibletravel.com

Dolphins-World - www.dolphins-world.com

Earth Observatory - www.earthobservatory.nasa.gov

España Spain's Official Tourism Website - www.spain.info

Euronews.Travel - www.euronews.com/travel

Going - www.going.com

Google - www.google.co.uk

Highway Logistics - www.highway-logistics.co.uk

Hotel Miramar Barcelona - hotelmiramarbarcelona.com

Housing Anywhere - www.housinganywhere.com

Interesting Engineering - www.interestingengineering.com

Isle of Wight Guru - www.isleofwightguru.co.uk

Kiddle - kids.kiddle.co

Marine Insight - www.marineinsight.com

Mobility at Sea - www.mobilityatsea.co.uk

Murcia Today - www.murciatoday.com

National Christmas Tree Association - www.realchristmastrees.org

National Geographic - www.nationalgeographic.co.uk

Navigate Content (Michelle Segrest) - www.navigatecontent.com

Oberlo - www.oberlo.com

On This Day - www.onthisday.com

Red Funnel - www.redfunnel.co.uk

Royal Museums Greenwich - www.rmg.co.uk

Sagrada Familia (Barcelona Tickets) - sagradafamilia.barcelona-tickets.com

Taylor UK - www.taylor-company.co.uk

The Bristorian - www.thebristorian.co.uk

The Manila Times - www.manilatimes.net

The Kitchn - www.thekitchn.com

The Sky Live - theskylive.com

Travel Dudes - www.traveldudes.com

Travel Feed (Juan Carlos Menendez) - www.travelfeed.com

UNESCO - www.unesco.org

Unofficial Royalty - www.unofficialroyalty.com

We World Experience - weareworldexperience.com

Website of Pascal Bonenfant - www.pascalbonenfant.com

Wikipedia - en.wikipedia.org

World Atlas - www.worldatlas.com

World History Encyclopaedia - www.worldhistory.org

1900s - www.1900s.org.uk

There are three other further sources of information, which are a little bit trickier to reference. These consist of:

A Short History of Spain and Portugal, courtesy of Stanford University's Aerospace Computing Laboratory - http://aero-comlab.stanford.edu/jameson/world_history/A_Short_History_of_Spain_and_Portugal.pdf

Tower of Hercules in Spain | History & Myths, by A Knapp (2023) for Study.com - study.com/academy/lesson/tower-of-hercules-history-mythology-location.html

When Place of Birth is at Sea, by M Jones (2018) for UW Applied Population Lab - *https://apl.wisc.edu/shared/tad/sea-birth#:~:text=For%20decades%2C%20citizenship%20in%20these,which%20the%20vessel%20is%20registered.*

COMING SOON.

TODDLER ON TOUR:
MOVING FJORD

If you have enjoyed **Toddler on Tour: Viva España**, please do tell as many people about it as you can. And if you really, *really* enjoyed it, please feel free to leave a little review.

The next riveting instalment to feature in this original series will be **Toddler on Tour: Moving Fjord**.

Join us as we set sail from Southampton aboard *P&O Cruises* Britannia to experience the mighty majesty of the Norwegian Fjords. To whet your appetite further still, here is a taster of what is to come: a chance to hop aboard what is rumoured to be the world's most scenic railway journey at Flåm; a journey to bring us up close and personal with the momentous Briksdal Glacier from Olden; a boat trip to look up at the Pulpit Rock on my birthday from Stavanger (ascending this sheer rock face is apparently not toddler friendly according to the parents), and; a nosy around the prominent Norwegian town with Viking roots that is Haugesund.

With a full compliment of gnashers, legs that are now designed for running and an ever-expanding vocabulary of both made-up and legitimate words, the possibilities for mayhem and mischief are growing with each and every passing day. I can't wait to share this sequel with you and look forward to your company.

All that's left for me to say is ¡adios España! and hallo Norge.

TODDLER ON TOUR:
MOVING FJORD

www.ingramcontent.com/pod-product-compliance
Ingram Content Group UK Ltd.
Pitfield, Milton Keynes, MK11 3LW, UK
UKHW012130260525
458932UK00003B/99

9 781803 819327